MASS CLASS

MASS CLASS

YOUR QUESTIONS
ANSWERED

FATHER DAVE DWYER

Host of *The Busted Halo Show*

Paulist Press
New York / Mahwah, NJ

Caseside image by Peter Murphy
Caseside and book design by Lynn Else

Library of Congress Cataloging-in-Publication Data
Names: Dwyer, Dave, author.
Title: Mass class : your questions answered / Father Dave Dwyer.
Description: New York / Mahwah, NJ : Paulist Press, [2022] | "Host of The Busted Halo Show." | Summary: "Join Father Dave Dwyer, host of the popular radio call-in The Busted Halo Show, for a regular segment dubbed "Mass Class"-in a handy book form"—Provided by publisher.
Identifiers: LCCN 2022005821 (print) | LCCN 2022005822 (ebook) | ISBN 9780809106660 (hardcover) | ISBN 9781587689383 (ebook)
Subjects: LCSH: Mass—Miscellanea. | Lord's Supper—Catholic Church—Miscellanea.
Classification: LCC BX2230.3 .D89 2022 (print) | LCC BX2230.3 (ebook) | DDC 264/.36—dc23/eng/20220511
LC record available at https://lccn.loc.gov/2022005821
LC ebook record available at https://lccn.loc.gov/2022005822

ISBN 978-0-8091-0666-0 (hardcover)
ISBN 978-1-58768-938-3 (e-book)

Published by Paulist Press
997 Macarthur Boulevard
Mahwah, New Jersey 07430
www.paulistpress.com

Printed and bound in Colombia
www.milibroimpreso.com

Dedicated to Frances W. Dwyer.
The strength of your faith continues to be
an inspiration to many.
PTL

Contents

Contents

Welcome to Mass Class

People have a lot of questions about Catholicism. Makes sense. The Church has been around a long time amassing a storehouse of theology that attempts to illuminate a transcendent God. It also stands to reason that Catholics would bring their questions to a priest. However, when I was new to the ordained ministry, it made me squirm when people would ask me questions about the faith, largely because I felt inadequate. "What do I know? I'm just a 'baby priest.' I don't know everything there is to know about the Catholic Church!"

Cut to twenty years later. Every weeknight, as a Catholic priest who's now also a talk radio show host, I answer questions of faith as they come in live on the phone. Some might call that "working without a net." But for me, *The Busted Halo Show with Father Dave Dwyer* on SiriusXM's The Catholic Channel has been fun and interesting every night for over fifteen years. Okay, *almost* every night. And while I never fancied myself a teacher, I am humbled when callers describe a lightbulb going on over their heads after hearing my attempt to answer their question. I would not have guessed at the start of my priestly ministry that this is where

I'd end up. God really knows how to persuade us to do things we are prone to resist.

I still don't know everything. But I have picked up one or two things along the way. And I know where to look when I come up empty. A customer service expert on a cruise line once taught me that when you don't know an answer, you should not say, "I don't know," but rather, "Let me find out for you." Wish I'd learned that one in seminary. I'm amazed that even today people still come up with questions I've not answered yet or even thought of myself. God bless the People of God!

This book is a compilation of questions on a particular topic, one that I often describe as our most common experience together as Catholics: the Mass. From the time our show first went on the air, we dubbed the middle day of the week "Mass Class Wednesday." Poring over thousands of hours of audio files, we managed to find quite a few questions I had answered about the Mass—many on Wednesdays, but on other days too. Nevertheless, I do not purport that this is an exhaustive book on everything one would need to know about the Catholic Mass. There are plenty of those out there, and they do a good job. What I like about what we've put together here is that these questions come from *you*. They were actually asked (some of them many times over) by real people who called or wrote into the show. And because of that, I'm pretty sure there are at least a few questions that don't appear in those other fine books. Now, we did choose to "change the names to protect the innocent"—as they used to announce at the beginning of every episode of the seminal 1950s police detective show *Dragnet*. So if you're a regular listener of the show and stumble upon a question that sounds like one you've asked, don't be disappointed if a name other than your own is credited as the source.

You will also notice a few questions labeled **TOP 5!** These are the five most frequently asked Mass Class questions in the history of the show (or at least some variation of the question included here). These are not necessarily the five most important or most controversial or most inspiring questions. For this ranking, we're just going by how often you asked them. When I was back in seminary, I probably wouldn't have guessed people would ask me these five questions most often as a priest, but ask them you did!

On something of a practical note, I've tried to keep the text streamlined without footnotes, so you'll notice my quoting almost exclusively from primary sources. This gives the book a more authentic feel to what listeners hear each night on the air because I'm not sitting in the midst of a vast theological library when hosting a radio show. Usually in the studio I have within arm's reach only the *Roman Missal* (the prayer book priests use during Mass), the Bible, and my pocket edition of the *Catechism of the Catholic Church*. Granted, the latter would really only fit in a pocket found in cargo pants in a Big & Tall store.

If you're new to reading material with churchy cross-references, I'll try to keep it simple. When you see *CCC* and a number, that is referring to the appropriate paragraph number from the *Catechism of the Catholic Church*, a handy summary and compilation of *almost* all Catholic teaching. Major Church documents tend to use paragraph numbers rather than page numbers because when something gets translated into different languages or printed by different publishers (or these days published digitally online) the page numbers will not match. The same is true when you see the abbreviation *GIRM* and a number. That stands for *The General Instruction of the Roman Missal*, which gives us the directions for how to celebrate the Catholic Mass, as well as offering the reasoning behind what we do. If you would like more information or care to see the full context of something I've quoted, you can acquire your own copies of these works or access any of them online for free. It might even make you feel like a theology student!

Permit me now a few acknowledgments. Some folks can sit down by themselves and just write a book. That has never been my gift. I have on occasion felt tuckered out after simply composing an email! This book, therefore, has been a very collaborative effort. It would not have come to fruition without the frequent encouragement of my brother Paulist, Father Mark-David Janus, CSP, president and publisher of Paulist Press. For the countless hours of listening, transcribing, and editing my at times stream-of-consciousness radio remarks into something legible in print form, I am grateful for the talents of Diane Vescovi, Trace Murphy, and Jennifer Sawyer Bogardus. There would be no audio to transcribe without the radio show I have been hosting nightly for over fifteen years. To the success of that ministry I owe much gratitude to Joe Zwilling, Robyn Gould, Brett Siddell, Christina Ambrosino, Adam Hamway, and countless others at SiriusXM Radio and the Catholic Channel who have not only kept us on the air but have been responsible for touching hearts and bringing people back to the faith. My thanks go also to the leadership of the Paulist Fathers, who have seen fit to allow me, a missionary, to remain in this media ministry for so long. Finally, I would not have much to say about the Mass if it were not for Msgr. Kevin W. Irwin and Father Andrew D. Ciferni, O.Praem., two of the finest liturgical mentors any priest could hope for. Thank you, one and all!

And now, on to answering your questions.
Let's go to the phones...

PART I

Why Go to Mass?

1. Do we have to go to church to pray to God?

2. Why is attending Mass an obligation for Catholics?

3. Yes, but why do we have to go on Sunday?

4. Is missing Mass really such a serious sin?

5. If I regularly cannot attend Sunday Mass because of my job, does it count if I listen to Mass on the radio?

6. Must I receive communion at Mass to fulfill my obligation?

7. What if I don't want to go to Mass because of the scandals?

1. Do we have to go to church to pray to God?

A friend who is Christian but not Catholic wonders why I can't just spend time in personal prayer or reading the Bible. He says God isn't only found in church. So why do we Catholics have to go to Mass?

Kathy in Bellaire, Texas

Your friend is right: God isn't only to be found inside a church. Many saints, popes, and preachers in our history have long encouraged people of faith to seek out and find God everywhere in the world around us. So no, Catholics don't believe that a church is the *only* place we can pray. But we do believe it's a very important place to pray. You see, it's less about the building per se and more about believers gathering together. Do you remember the movie *Field of Dreams* with Kevin Costner, and that iconic whispered line: "If you build it, they will come"? The point is not construction; the essential thing is people *coming together*. The church acts as a locus for one of the most central tenets of Christianity: creating community.

Here's something to discuss with your Christian friend. All throughout the Bible God interacts with his people *communally*. Yes, there are a handful of unique times when God appears or speaks to an individual. But none of those are merely for the sake of that individual. In the Old Testament, God establishes a covenant with all the Israelites, as a nation. In the New Testament, Jesus calls disciples and empowers them to preach to and heal great numbers of people. Essentially, Jesus's entire ministry is teaching us that love isn't about *me*, it's about *others*.

Only in the last two hundred years has there been a shift in many Christian traditions toward individual salvation and believers having a "personal relationship" with Jesus Christ. By and large, that is not what we see in the Scriptures. God didn't have all of those conversations with Moses on the top of a mountain just so that Moses himself could deepen his own faith in God. After our Lord called the disciples in the Gospels, he did not set up one-on-one meetings with them. His followers experienced the miracles and teaching of Jesus together as a community.

Simply put, Catholicism is not a me-and-Jesus religion; it's a *We*-and-Jesus religion. *We* are the Body of Christ. St. Paul goes to great pains in his writings to teach us that the body is a cohesive unit and that it would be foolish for the individual parts of the body to think that they can go it alone or that they are disconnected from the whole (see 1 Corinthians 12:12–27). Going to church helps to reinforce that.

Could we be reminded that we are part of a community in other ways? Sure. But Catholics believe in sacramentality, that is to say that we experience God and our faith through all of our human senses. So, if at the cornerstone of our faith is being part of a community of believers—many of whom are different from me, some of whom I might disagree with or find annoying—how do we best bring that to life: by being alone and thinking about all those other people, or by having them physically surround us in the pews?

It seems to me that one of the major lessons of the recent global pandemic is how much people desire—even need—to gather together in person. Many Catholics reported sorely missing not only receiving communion but also coming together with their fellow parishioners on a regular basis. This is an example of how the Church's wisdom is reinforced by our human experience. Gathering together as a community is not just a rule for its own sake: it is good for us to come together, and the Church wants what's good for us!

2. Why is attending Mass an obligation for Catholics?

My fiancée doesn't understand why Catholics need to go to Mass every Sunday or why we call it an "obligation." She thinks we should go if we want to. What should I tell her?

Andrew in North Tustin, California

Let's start with something humans don't often react well to. Remember back when you were a kid and you asked, "But *why*, Mom, why do I *have* to do that?" Likely one of her go-to responses was, "Because I said so." Same here, except the "I" in this case is God. Back when God first started making himself known to us humans, as described in the first few books of the Bible, he gave us commandments. These were top-level important things like, "Don't murder people." Also among these nonnegotiables was "Make sure that every week you take time out from your busy schedule to remember that I alone am God" (see Exodus 20:1–11). Jesus, just before dying on the cross so that despite our sins we can have eternal life, gathered his followers around a table, shared a meal with them, and commanded them to "do this in memory of me." In the Ten Commandments God tells us we need to stop for some "holy time" weekly. In the Gospels, Jesus demonstrates what that holy time should look like. So we Catholics consider it an obligation to take time out every Sunday to come together around the table of the Lord *because God said so.*

Okay, but by the time we're adults, Mom's "because I said so" usually isn't sufficient to motivate us to action. So what if we substitute the word *commitment* for *obligation*? I have a friend who wakes up at the crack of dawn every day to do some sort of punishing Crossfit-type of exercise class. She'll often post to social media sweaty, red-faced selfies and tell the tale of how the class kicked her butt. She'd be the first to admit she doesn't *like* going to this class, and there are plenty of days that she doesn't *want* to go. But she's *committed* to going because she sees the value in exercise on a regular basis—for her own personal health and as a motivation to others in her life. Commitments almost always involve some sacrifice, but we deem those to be worth it because what we are committed to is of a higher value.

For instance, if we are *committed* to our family, we feel an *obligation* to be around the family table at thanksgiving or for a significant birthday. Why does a family impose unspoken obligations like this (or even spoken ones) for important occasions? Because gathering together, being present to one another, is part of what it means to be a family. As Catholics, the Church is our family. If our commitment to our faith is genuine, then obligation and sacrifice will naturally flow from it.

3. Yes, but why do we have to go on Sunday?

I agree with the concept of carving out time for God each week. But Sunday is really busy for our family: the kids have soccer practice. Mass is offered at their Catholic school every Friday. That's once a week–shouldn't that count?

Patricia in Springfield, Massachusetts

Weekday Masses are not the same as Sunday Masses and do not fulfill our Sunday obligation as Catholics. Why? Quite simply because Sunday is the day that Jesus rose from the dead. It is the day of the week when the possibility of eternal life, life after death, became a reality for the human race. We believe that because of something that happened on a Sunday anyone who believes may indeed have their own resurrection and be with God in heaven forever. That's actually a pretty big deal.

It may seem that in our busy modern lives lots of things are priorities. So many activities fill up our week. But if we take a step back and think about it, what is more important in the life of our family than Christ's gift to us of everlasting life?

In the immediate aftermath of Jesus's death, resurrection,

and ascension, the first Christians decided very early on that Sunday would henceforth be considered "the Lord's Day," and that would be the day each week that the community would gather to celebrate the "breaking of the bread" in memory of him. The vast majority of them were originally Jewish by birth and very familiar with the Old Testament concept of the Sabbath. They would not have questioned the value of a single agreed upon day every week when all of God's people would put aside the other things they had to do and gather for communal prayer. For thousands of years that day of the week had been Saturday. With Jesus's initiating the new covenant in his own blood, those first-century Christians chose to transform that weekly religious observance from the Sabbath (Saturday) to the Lord's Day (Sunday). In the two millennia since, those who believe that Christ's death and resurrection has gifted us with the hope of eternal life have put aside other commitments on Sundays to come together and give thanks for this gift (see *CCC* 2175–78).

Now, I realize that decision was made a long time ago and none of us twenty-first-century folk got to vote on it. Nor does the pope send around a Doodle poll every so often to see which day of the week works best for all the Catholics on the planet. If this were some other global brand or institution that wanted "buy in" from 1.2 billion people, they'd probably do market research every year to see which hour of which day works best for most of us. But we're not a big corporation trying to make it convenient for its customers. We're the Church founded by Jesus Christ, who rose from the dead on a Sunday. So, I'll see you this Sunday in church, okay?

mass class notes

Catechism of the Catholic Church: a single-volume summary and compilation of Catholic teachings and beliefs

9

4. Is missing Mass really such a serious sin?

I find myself on occasion, sad to say, missing Mass, but it is rare. Is it really so serious?

Tony in Oswego, Illinois

Well, it depends. The Church does consider missing Sunday Mass to be a serious (or "mortal") sin. But first let me underscore that we're only talking about *Sunday* Mass here. Catholics are not required to attend Mass on weekdays (with the rare exception of a handful of "holy days of obligation" that may fall during the week, like Christmas). Even then the Church allows us to miss Mass on a Sunday or holy day *for a good reason*. OK, so what's a "good reason"?

If Sunday comes along and I find myself in the hospital hooked up to an IV and I miss Mass, that's very different from me lying on the couch watching March Madness basketball. In both cases I miss Mass, but the Church makes a distinction; one is a sin, the other is not. Just like in civil law, intent and culpability are important. If your elderly mother's health-care aide had to cancel at the last minute on a Sunday and you can't leave your mom unattended, you don't need to confess missing Mass that day as a grave sin. During the summer, if you and your kids prefer to get to the pool first thing on Sunday morning to grab the best lounge chairs, you best find your way to the confession line, because I think we can safely say that doesn't meet the "good reason" criteria.

When we gather together in community to celebrate the Eucharist, we are doing what Christ said to do in memory of him, and those words of Christ are important (see Luke 22:19). He didn't say, "Do this in memory of me if it works well with your schedule." Or "Do this in memory of me unless it's a holiday weekend." Or "Do this in memory of me, but only if your pastor is a really dynamic preacher."

Things come up that are out of our control, and there's no need to get overly scrupulous about that. But if we're choosing to say, "I just don't want to go. I know it's wrong, but I'm going to choose not to go," then that's a serious sin.

One last thing. The way you asked the question makes it sound as though you might be tempted to adopt an attitude like, "Hey, I go to church way more Sundays than I miss. Can't I just get a pass every *once in a while*?" Well, that would be like saying to the police officer who pulls you over for running a red light, "Officer, I'm usually pretty good about stopping at red lights. Can't I get a pass on this one? Am I really expected to stop at every single red light?" I'll let you imagine his response.

5. If I regularly cannot attend Sunday Mass because of my job, does it count if I listen to Mass on the radio?

I'm an over-the-road truck driver and my schedule doesn't permit me to attend church on a regular basis. When I mentioned this to another Catholic truck driver, he said if we fail to make our Sunday obligation, it's a mortal sin. What if I listen to Mass on the radio, does that count?

Daniel, driving through Tennessee

Over many years of hosting this show, I've learned a lot about the life and work of you truck drivers, and let me start by saying, "Thank you!" You make it possible for the rest of us to get everything we order online delivered right to our door in a timely manner. And I know you make many sacrifices for that—for us. Those sacrifices include being away from your families for weeks on end, not being able to predict exactly when you will be where, and missing out on much of life at home, including Catholic parish life.

I've heard other truckers say, "This is my job. I'm not in charge of my schedule and that means some weeks I have to work on Sunday." What you do for a living can make it hard for you to get to Mass. And you're not alone. I'm thinking of the many other shift workers, like nurses who will sometimes be at the hospital for twenty-four hours straight. Or people that work in retail or the restaurant industry, for whom Sunday is not only not a day off, but it can be one of the busiest workdays. Because avoiding working on Sunday has become less possible for people in our modern culture, the Church has responded with changes like allowing Sunday Masses to be celebrated starting on Saturday evening—in most dioceses often as early as 4:00 p.m.—and in many places extending the "window of opportunity" through Sunday evening or even Sunday night. I used to work at a parish in New York City that was smack in the middle of the Theater District. The pastor added a Mass to their schedule very late on Saturday night so that performers, stagehands, and theatergoers could attend Mass after the Broadway shows ended. So the Church is aware of the challenges of those who work on Sundays and is trying to do everything it can to make it possible for you to still be able to fulfill your Sunday obligation.

Another way of saying that, albeit more negatively, is that the Church is trying to make it so that fewer people have an excuse to miss Mass. Sure, lots of people end up having to work on Sunday. But a much smaller number are stuck at work from 4:00 p.m. on Saturday all the way through to 8:00 p.m. on Sunday. And modern technology has made it fairly easy to find a church near you that has a Mass time that will fit your schedule. What I typically say to many Sunday workers is, "Are you sure you really can't make it to any Mass offered by parishes in your area at some point on the weekend?" Because if it's possible but not particularly convenient, then the Church would consider choosing not to go to be a sin.

However, in the case of you truckers, there are many more factors that impinge upon your ability to get to Mass. If you're driving a long haul on a Sunday, even if it is possible for you to take time off and find a Catholic Church for Mass, you often can't park your rig in or near the church parking lot, and getting a ride from the closest truck stop may be cost prohibitive or very difficult to arrange. I have heard of certain Catholic parishes along major trucking routes that have volunteers to pick truckers up at a truck stop and drive them to the church and back, but those are by no means common.

So, Daniel, if your job really does prevent you from attending Sunday Mass, that is not a mortal sin because mortal sin is always something that we freely choose to do, not something out of our control. It sounds to me like the desire in your heart is to go to Mass and that's really what the obligation is about (see *CCC* 2181). You asked about listening to Mass on the radio. I highly recommend that! You'll derive a great many spiritual benefits by hearing the Word of God proclaimed and preached, and by joining in with the prayers that you hear. But does it "count" as fulfilling your Sunday obligation? No, it does not. Again, you're not committing a mortal sin if you genuinely cannot attend Mass, so strictly speaking it does not need to "count."

Daniel: "Thank you, Father. I feel so much better now!"

6. Must I receive communion at Mass to fulfill my obligation?

If I go to church on Sunday but do not receive communion, am I still fulfilling my obligation as a Catholic?

Debbie in Grand Island, Nebraska

The Sunday Mass obligation does not require us to receive the Eucharist. In fact, for the vast majority of the history of the Church it was not the common practice for people to receive communion every week. At the start of the twentieth century, Pope Pius X wrote to all the Catholics of the world encouraging more frequent reception of communion. And after the reforms of the Second Vatican Council in the 1960s, it became much more common to see pretty much the entire congregation getting out of the pews to go up and receive the Eucharist. So, for hundreds of years before that, Catholics who went to Mass but didn't receive were still fulfilling their Sunday obligation.

What we are required to do by our Mother, the Church, is take time out from our daily lives, come together, worship God in community, and be there for one another. We are not obliged to receive communion each time we go to Mass. But I would be remiss if I didn't say this: if you are not going up in the communion line because you are aware of a grave sin, then make some time to celebrate the sacrament of reconciliation with your priest. Confession is life for the soul!

mass class notes

Second Vatican Council (1962-65): a series of meetings of all the world's bishops that, among other things, made significant changes to the Catholic Mass for the first time in four hundred years

7. What if I don't want to go to Mass because of the scandals?

I am so disenchanted with the Catholic Church, especially in the area of all the scandals over the past twenty years. It makes me not even want to go to Mass because it all seems so corrupt. How do I keep the faith?

Nora in Franklin Park, Pennsylvania

Nora, I fully understand your reaction and quite honestly share your feelings. I myself have been sad, disillusioned, and angry that we as a Church have lost the trust of the people who we are charged with protecting, loving, pastoring, and educating. That is enormously damaging to the Body of Christ, to all Catholics throughout the world. We have tragically done great harm. It is heartbreaking for me to hear how most victims of priestly sexual abuse continue to live broken lives—and even more so to realize how many have taken their own lives. Also tragic is the reality that a great many people have been turned off to the faith because of the sins of some of my brother priests.

When the watershed story of clerical sexual abuse first broke in the *Boston Globe* in 2002, I had only been a priest for two years, and it really rocked my world. It was the first time the dark underbelly of the institutional Church and hierarchy became real for me. I questioned what I was a part of. I did not feel proud to be a member of this brotherhood that is called by God to serve his people, and that was very difficult. Yet even in those dark times I found myself clinging to an enduring truth.

When I was in college, my very wise campus minister, Father Charles Borgognoni, used to frequently say something I will always remember: "Never let a Catholic spoil your Catholicism." At the time, he was not speaking directly to the issue of the sexual abuse scandals, nor am I suggesting this phrase be used as a salve for abuse victims. Nonetheless, there is pervading wisdom in his injunction, particularly when it comes to the Church hierarchy: every one of us Catholics is an imperfect, damaged, fallible sinner, but our Catholic faith is bigger and holier than any one person or group of us. I hear Father Charlie's voice echoing in my head whenever I hear of Catholics causing harm—even bishops or other leaders—and I refuse to let their actions spoil my Catholic faith.

For some reason, Jesus chose to entrust his Church to us flawed human beings when he handed the keys over to St. Peter two thousand years ago (see Matthew 16:18–19). You might at times question that decision—I know I have! After all, throughout history, there have been many things done in the name of God that we should rightly be ashamed of. Yet Jesus also left us the Holy Spirit, and thank God for that! I'm convinced that if the Church's survival relied solely upon its human leaders, it would have disappeared centuries ago. We seem to keep shooting ourselves in the foot. But the Church is truly the People of God and God is still ultimately its protector.

Many people have called into our show and said things like, "I am appalled by what some priests did and angry about bishops trying to cover it up, but my faith is in Jesus. And as a Catholic, I believe Jesus is truly present in the Eucharist. So, I'm choosing to still go to Mass because even the actions of those sinful clergy are not going to keep me away from the sacrament. I need to be receiving Jesus now more than ever!" I couldn't agree more and couldn't have said it better.

So, Nora, you are not alone in your struggle. And while I know it will be difficult to be at Mass and see a priest up on the altar, I invite you to see Jesus there as well, present among us who have gathered around his table. Also, take a look to your left and your right when you're sitting in the pews. See those many other people who share your pain and frustration; pray for their faith and their healing as well as your own. Maybe they can serve as a reminder that "the Church" is not simply the ordained hierarchy, but more importantly the People of God. And please don't forget to pray for the people whose lives have been most affected by the sexual abuse scandal: the victims and their families.

PART 2

The Holy Eucharist

8. Do Catholics really believe it is Christ's flesh and blood we receive at communion?

9. At what point do the bread and wine become the Body and Blood of Christ?

10. Why is a small piece of host dropped into the chalice?

11. For how long after consecration does it remain the Body and Blood of Christ?

12. Is the host in the monstrance changed often, or is it always that same one?

13. Must we use red wine for communion, or is white okay?

14. Why does the priest add water into the chalice of wine?

15. Does the chalice get washed with soap after communion?

8. Do Catholics really believe it is Christ's flesh and blood we receive at communion?

One thing I find hard to wrap my head around as a Catholic: Do we actually believe that what we are receiving at communion is really the flesh and blood of Jesus Christ himself?

Juliette in Guelph, Ontario, Canada

The Catholic Church teaches that Christ is really and truly present in the Eucharist: body, blood, soul, and divinity. This is sometimes referred to as the "True Presence" or the "Real Presence." This term underscores that at Mass we are not merely mimicking what Jesus did at the Last Supper and using bread and wine as props as one would in a stage play. During the worship services of many other Christian denominations, believers will often ritually enact the Last Supper because Jesus did say, "Do this in memory of me." In most cases, though, other Christians do not believe that any miraculous change occurs while they're doing that.

In the Gospel of John, Jesus states emphatically, over and over again, that unless we eat his flesh and drink his blood we will not have eternal life within us. He says, "My flesh is true food, and my blood is true drink" (John 6:55). So, yes, we believe that during communion we are really receiving the flesh and blood of Christ. How can that be, you may ask, since it doesn't look or taste like human flesh or blood, but rather seems much more like it's still bread and wine?

The *Catechism of the Catholic Church* describes it this way: "Because Christ our Redeemer said that it was truly his body that he was offering…[we believe] that by the consecration of the bread and wine there takes place a change of the whole substance of the bread into the substance of the Body of Christ our Lord and of the whole substance of the wine into the substance of his blood. This change [we call] transubstantiation" (*CCC* 1376).

What's important to focus on here is the word "substance." The Church uses that term intentionally and in a somewhat technical sense. The *substance* of a thing is that which is most important in defining who or what it is. A good synonym might be the *essence* of something. In Greek philosophy, which Catholic theology builds upon, this essence or substance is distinct from the *outer material form* of something—one of these can change without the other changing.

Let's use a real-world example. Imagine someone whom you had not seen in a long time had dyed his hair and lost a lot of weight. Your first impression might be that this person is now very different. But after talking with him for a few minutes, everything sounds familiar. "Yup, this is the same old guy that I used to know, even if he looks quite different on the outside." Now imagine the opposite. You encounter another old friend after several years and marvel at how she hasn't aged a day. "It's amazing, you look the same!" Then she tells you about a life-changing event that happened to her. You notice that her whole perspective on the world has shifted substantially. Maybe she had a brush with death but survived, and she is noticeably a more grateful or compassionate person. You think, "This is not the same person I used to know." On the outside, her looks are indistinguishable from before; her voice sounds the same. But *on the inside,* a fundamental change has taken place. And unlike the hair dye that will eventually grow out, the life-changing event has had a permanent effect; there's no going back to the way things used to be. This is most akin to what we Catholics call transubstantiation.

What we believe happens to the bread and wine during Mass is this kind of change. Our senses cannot perceive a difference. The little round wheat wafer still looks, smells, and tastes the same; it's the same size and shape. But that which is most fundamental to its existence, the very essence of it, has been changed into the True Presence of Christ's flesh. A cynic might counter, "Well, isn't it convenient that you believe in this miraculous change that cannot be measured by science?" To which I'd respond, "Don't humans believe in other imperceptible concepts like love and truth and beauty?" We do, and we take them for granted, or if you will, take them on faith. The great twelfth-century theologian St. Thomas Aquinas put it this way: "That in this sacrament are the true Body of Christ and his true Blood is something that 'cannot be apprehended by the senses, but only by faith, which relies on divine authority'" (*CCC* 1381).

So, yes, we are truly receiving Christ's flesh and blood in communion, fulfilling his command.

9. At what point do the bread and wine become the Body and Blood of Christ?

I know that before Mass we have bread and wine, and by the time we get to communion they have become the Body and Blood of the Lord. But at what point in the Mass does this change actually happen?

Jerry in Cockeysville, Maryland

In some championship sporting competitions, the difference between the best in the world and second place can often be 1/100th of a second. We love to watch the slow-motion instant replay and freeze the exact frame when the swimmer touches the wall or the runner breaks the tape. Yes, thanks to modern technology, we can achieve infinitesimal precision on many things. But I'm not so sure Christ's miraculous presence in the Eucharist should be one of them.

One of my clearest memories from when I was in "Mass Class" (during my seminary years) is the professor emphasizing to us future priests that it is the entirety of the Mass that allows the

Lord to be truly present to us at communion. Certainly the words Jesus uttered at the Last Supper ("this is my body which will be given up for you") are indispensable, but also crucial is the action of the Holy Spirit that the priest overtly invites during a prayer called the epiclesis ("Let your spirit come upon these gifts to make them holy"), and even the response and acclamations of the gathered assembly are necessary. Christ becomes sacramentally present during our celebration of the Mass, the whole Mass. In a sense, it would be a mistake to look for a more precise moment because we might be tempted to limit the value of the sacrament to a small portion of the Mass, or liken a few lines to some magical incantation that, when said, summon our God from the heavens. This sacrament is powerful and mysterious, but it's not a Michael Keaton movie where the characters say "Beetlejuice" three times and voila, he appears.

In fact, the reality is, even in an emergency such as running out of consecrated hosts, no priest or bishop or even the pope can just quickly run back into the sacristy and consecrate some more by simply repeating one part of the Eucharistic Prayer. One can't even legitimately celebrate just the second half of the Mass that begins after homily. It's a package deal!

Having said all that, you are correct: before Mass it's just bread and wine, but when we receive communion it's the True Presence of the Lord. So, it's at least fair to want to narrow down the timeline a little bit. Okay, so let's focus on one ritual action during the Eucharistic Prayer. Following the words of institution (the very words Jesus spoke at the Last Supper that we believe "instituted" this sacrament), "Take this, all of you, and eat of it, for this is my body, which will be

mass class notes

Sacristy:
"backstage" room where things are prepared and priests get ready for Mass

given up for you," the priest holds the host up in the air and then genuflects in adoration. He then does the same with the chalice after pronouncing Christ's words about his blood. The stark visual of the priest pausing in silence to elevate the host and then the chalice, along with his profound gesture of getting down on one knee immediately following, clearly indicate that our Lord is now sacramentally present in the Eucharist. After all, your priest would not be genuflecting to mere bread or wine. So, we can conclude that at some point between the words "Let your spirit come upon these gifts" (the epiclesis) and the act of genuflection, the transubstantiation has occurred.

The *Catechism of the Catholic Church* seems also to leave the question somewhat open. In one place it sounds like it's offering exactitude: "The Eucharistic presence of Christ begins at the moment of the consecration and endures as long as the Eucharistic species subsist" (*CCC* 1377). Yet, when speaking more broadly about the Mass, it declares, "At the heart of the Eucharistic celebration are the bread and wine that, by the words of Christ *and the invocation of the Holy Spirit*, become Christ's Body and Blood" (*CCC* 1333, emphasis added). This seems to reinforce that at a minimum *both* the epiclesis and words of institution are responsible for the transubstantiation. Even the more specific of those two passages allows for some ambiguity as the *Catechism* does not define what the "moment of consecration" actually is. Is it the first syllable of the institution narrative? The last? Is it a brief moment? A long one that began at the epiclesis? Perhaps. Maybe.

Another term for the Mass is the *Sacred Mysteries*. Let's resist our modern proclivity for frame-by-frame precision timing and leave room for some of the mystery of God during the Mass. All we really need to know is that Christ is truly present—body, blood, soul, and divinity—in the Eucharist by the time we are in the communion line. Our response when the minister says, "The Body of Christ" is not, "Hey Jesus, when did you get here?" but rather, "Amen": "I believe."

10. Why is a small piece of host dropped into the chalice?

Every time I'm at Mass I notice that the priest drops a small piece of the host into one of the chalices, and I've always wondered why he does this.

Sheila in Broomfield, Colorado

Like all good symbolic actions, this one has multiple levels of meaning. Upon observing the priest drop a small piece of the host into the chalice, we may recall a significant theological principle: Catholics believe that Christ is present body, blood, soul, and divinity in *each and both* of the "Eucharistic species," the consecrated bread and wine (see *CCC* 1377). This ritual act does not cause this to happen, but rather serves as a visual reminder.

The original meaning of this gesture is entirely different, however, and the history behind it is actually a fascinating story! I was reminded of this historical tidbit while watching the 2020 Emmy Awards ceremony on TV. Because of the coronavirus pandemic, all of the nominees were participating in the ceremony via videoconference from their homes rather than gathering in person in a single large theater. The producers dispatched to every nominee's house minions in hazmat costumes holding an actual Emmy statue, ready to be awarded. When the winner was announced, their doorbell would ring and they'd be handed the Emmy in person. (Of course, only the winners were given a trophy, so in what must have been a huge tease for many nominees, those who did not win had to watch the hazmat-clad minion turn around and head back to Hollywood, undelivered Emmy in hand.) But the point is that because not everybody could gather in the same place in person, a great effort was made to bring the most vital and tangible part of the ceremony to all the remote places where people actually were.

Sixteen hundred years prior to that telecast, the leader of the Catholic Church had an idea to do something similar. Up until that point most Romans would come together on Sundays for the pope's Mass. As the Church grew, this became less feasible, so Pope Innocent I began the practice of consecrating extra bread at his Mass and then sending out a band of ministers to deliver this papal Eucharist to parishes all over Rome. The parish priest would then drop the consecrated morsel from the pope into his chalice just before communion. This way, the People of God could feel they were still participating in the pope's Mass, even from their remote locations. This simple practice, called "commingling," solidified the unity of the Church—not just unity with the pope himself, but also unity with all those other parishes practicing the same ritual.

Today we preserve this practice that complements the many other prayers said during the Mass that seek to bring about the unity of all God's people.

11. For how long after consecration does it remain the Body and Blood of Christ?

I was speaking with a friend who was unsure how long the effects of the consecration lasted. So, Father Dave, how long do the bread and wine stay the Body and Blood of Christ?

Hilary in Rapid City, South Dakota

It's a permanent change. Some other Christian traditions hold a similar belief to ours that the bread changes into the presence of the Lord, but for only as long as that particular congregation is still gathered together in the church. In their view, when people disperse after the service is over, it reverts to being bread. We however believe that once the elements are consecrated, they stay changed (see *CCC* 1377).

Remember that our Catholic doctrine of transubstantiation means that a fundamental change to the very essence of that which was once merely bread has occurred during the Eucharistic Prayer.

This change is perpetual—even more permanent than a tattoo because if you really, really regret it, the ink on your forearm can indeed be removed. You can't use a laser to morph the Eucharist back into being just bread; what's done is done.

We hold that the True Presence of Christ remains. That's why we have tabernacles in Catholic churches, because we believe we should continue to show respect and reverence to the Body of Christ by reserving it in a special place (as opposed to it going back into the cabinet in the sacristy alongside the unconsecrated hosts that are stored in cardboard boxes or Tupperware). The *General Instruction of the Roman Missal* directs that "the Most Blessed Sacrament should be reserved in a tabernacle in a part of the church that is truly noble, prominent, readily visible, beautifully decorated, and suitable for prayer" (*GIRM* 314).

mass class notes

Eucharistic Prayer: longest prayer of the Mass, which includes giving God thanks, calling upon the Holy Spirit, and consecrating the bread and wine (for more, see question 16 in part 3)

The tabernacle has two main purposes, both of which point to the belief that Christ remains permanently present in the Eucharist: (1) to contain "extra" consecrated hosts that may be brought to the sick or homebound later on; and (2) so that anytime the church is open to visitors, believers may have the opportunity to pray in the presence of the Lord (see *CCC* 1379). The latter we usually refer to as adoration of Christ in the Blessed Sacrament. Since Christians only adore or worship God, God must still be present in the Eucharist—otherwise we'd be committing the sin of idolatry by adoring little wafers of bread.

As a side note, not that you asked: only the consecrated hosts are reserved in the tabernacle. We never retain any of the Precious

Blood once Mass is over, but rather always consume however much we consecrate at any given Mass. That's not to say that we think the change to the wine is any less permanent. Rather, it's just never been Catholic tradition (mostly for practical reasons) to reserve consecrated wine after Mass.

Having said all that, Hilary, if you will allow me to recast slightly what you're asking…perhaps a more spiritual question might be, After Mass, how long do we who receive Christ remain changed or affected by our reception of the sacrament? Is ours a permanent change as well, or does it fade? Maybe we can just pray that our communion with the Lord has a positive effect on us at least as long as it takes to get out of the church parking lot!

12. Is the host in the monstrance changed often, or is it always that same one?

I enjoy spending time in prayer before the Blessed Sacrament when my parish offers a few hours of adoration on Fridays. But I've sometimes wondered, how long does that host stay in the monstrance before it needs to be changed, or is it always that same host?

Krista in Portland, Oregon

Well, first of all, the host doesn't usually stay in the monstrance for very long. It's really only in there during adoration and benediction. Most monstrances have a removable part, called a lunette, which is some combination of glass and metal that is just large enough to hold one of the three-inch diameter hosts. It is easily slipped out of the monstrance and placed in the church's tabernacle until the next time it is needed for adoration. The exception to this would be churches that have perpetual adoration. In that case, the host would in fact remain in the monstrance all the time, perpetually.

Yet your question remains: How much time goes by before the host is changed out with a newly consecrated one?

Let's get this out of the way: it is not the same host month after month, year after year. Our belief in transubstantiation holds that the consecrated host contains the Real Presence of Jesus Christ while retaining the same physical properties of bread. Therefore, it could get moldy if left in there too long, so it's consumed out of reverence and replaced with a freshly consecrated host periodically. I'm sure it varies from parish to parish, but I'd bet most change it about once a week.

Fear not, just like the sticker on the inside of your windshield that reminds you of when to change your oil, the church sacristan—the behind-the-scenes staff member or volunteer who takes care of setting up for and cleaning up after Mass—will likely have some system for making sure the host in the lunette is swapped out for a new one on a regular basis.

13. Must we use red wine for communion, or is white okay?

I was a little shocked when I discovered my parish uses white wine for communion. When I was growing up, I remember it always being red wine. Is it okay to use white?

Dustin in Baton Rouge, Louisiana

Yes, it is perfectly okay to use white wine. In my experience, it's a great deal less common, but in no way less acceptable. The only requirement the Church has is that the wine used must be made from grapes by natural fermentation, without any artificial additives, such as preservatives or flavors (see *Code of Canon Law* 924). This means it must actually be wine (and not merely grape juice, as some other Christian churches use for their communion services) with an alcohol content commensurate with industry standards, usually a minimum of 5 percent alcohol by volume. Another implication from these criteria is that rice wine, common throughout much of Asia, may not be used for communion.

A priest in recovery from alcoholism may request special permission from his bishop to use something called mustum, which is produced by a process that bypasses fermentation and therefore has no alcohol content. This is only granted on a case-by-case basis and only applies to the priest's chalice. He would also need to consecrate other chalices with regular wine if the Precious Blood is to be offered to the congregation.

Okay, but really your question is about the color. Even though there is no preference shown in Church law, one could make an argument that red wine is a fuller expression of the sacramental sign since we believe it will become Christ's blood, and blood is of course red. True, but this reasoning falls short when it comes to the other Eucharistic species: a small round bleached-white host is in no way visually similar to the flesh of a first-century Jew from Palestine. Or one might ask, which wine did Christ offer at the Last Supper: white or red? While it is strongly likely, because of Jewish tradition, that Jesus would have used red wine, there is historical evidence that white wine was somewhat common in the Roman Empire around that time as well. So we can't really know for sure.

One person who is very likely in favor of using white wine for communion: whoever is responsible for cleaning the purificators, those white napkin-like cloths that are used to wipe the Chalice after each person receives. As you can imagine, it is no small task to remove red wine stains from white linen or cotton. Using white wine makes their job a lot easier!

When it comes to a meal, I'm more of a red wine guy. I like a nice Italian or French red at a special occasion dinner. But at Mass, I have no personal preference, and neither does the Church.

14. Why does the priest add water into the chalice of wine?

Someone asked me the other day, "Why does the priest put water in with the wine before the consecration?" I guessed it had to do with the blood and water that flowed from Jesus's side when he was pierced. Is that right?

Veronica in Odessa, Texas

It is! Well…actually, that's only part of the answer, so let's fill out the rest. As with many of our ritual actions during Mass, often there are theological underpinnings, as well as practical reasons for their use.

First, let's recap what happens in the ritual you're referring to. During the offertory part of the Mass, which begins the Liturgy of the Eucharist, the priest adds a few drops of water to the chalice of wine (see *GIRM* 142). As a quick aside, when multiple chalices are used, he need only add water to one of them—even though putting water in all the chalices is fairly common practice. Historically, the reason for adding some water to the wine—and you might chuckle at this—is that people in the ancient Near East would hardly ever drink wine without diluting it with water, because it was often a little strong or wasn't very good tasting. They were watering it down to make it palatable. Today that's no longer an issue and so the symbolic meaning of the gesture takes precedence.

mass class notes

Liturgy of the Eucharist: roughly the second half of Mass, primarily consisting of consecrating the bread and wine and distributing communion

Seeing water being mixed with wine that will soon be the blood of Jesus rightly reminded you of when the soldier pierced Jesus's side with a lance after he died on the cross and both blood and water flowed from his side (see John 19:34). You're right: this ritual is strongly reminiscent of that scene. But let's dig a little bit deeper.

Accompanying the water-wine mixing is a short prayer, one you most likely wouldn't hear because there's typically music playing and a collection being taken up at this time. The prayer is, "By the mystery of this water and wine, may we come to share in the divinity of Christ, who humbled himself to share in our humanity." This is a great example of when the words of the prayer teach us about the purpose of what goes along with them. Here the Church is choosing to highlight the doctrine of the two natures of Christ. We believe that Jesus Christ is 100 percent human and 100 percent divine—not 50/50, and not sometimes God and sometimes a man (see *CCC* 464–69). So the wine represents the divine nature of Christ and the water represents his human nature.

The prayer (one of my favorites in the Mass), however, goes further than merely pointing out Christ's two natures. The part about our Lord humbling himself might call to mind that powerful passage from Paul's letter to the Philippians:

Though [Christ Jesus] was in the form of God,
he did not regard equality with God something to be
    grasped.
Rather, he emptied himself,
taking the form of a slave,
coming in human likeness;
and found human in appearance,
he humbled himself,
    becoming obedient to death,
    even death on a cross. (Philippians 2:6–8)

But wait, that's not all! Because Christ "shared in our humanity," we who believe will one day get to "share in Christ's divinity." Let's be clear: this is not all of us becoming our own individual gods. But it certainly sounds like more than merely us getting to *observe* Christ's divine nature once we get to heaven. No, we actually *share* in the divinity of Christ! I love that prayer.

15. Does the chalice get washed with soap after communion?

After we have all drunk from the chalice at communion, is it cleaned thoroughly with hot water and dish soap over at the rectory? I see my priest use a small cloth to wipe it down during Mass, but I hope that's not all that's done to clean it.

Peggy in Silver City, New Mexico

The chalice is what we call "purified" by the priest or deacon during Mass, immediately following the communion rite. The *General Instruction of the Roman Missal* directs that he does this without leaving the sanctuary area, either right on the altar or at a little side table called a credence table (see *GIRM* 163). The purification process goes like this: The priest or deacon pours some water into the chalice, swishes it around so as to pick up any drops of Christ's Precious Blood clinging to the inside, and then drinks it all. Next, he wipes the chalice thoroughly with a purificator, a special cloth blessed for this purpose, which has a little cross usually sewn right into the fabric so we know this is no ordinary napkin. Okay, that's the ritual cleansing of the chalice, but is that all? Is it considered all clean now? Not necessarily.

Following Mass, the chalice is usually taken back into the sacristy (the backstage set-up room) where it is cleaned again with soap and water or other disinfectant. Kind of like when you're watching a cooking show…the host makes some attempt to clean up their mess while they're talking to the camera, but we all know that after the credits roll, the production staff performs the real cleanup effort in the less pretty sink off the set.

And here's a cool inside scoop for you: almost all Catholic church sacristies have a special "sacred sink" that drains directly into the ground, as opposed to into the sewer system of the local community. This *sacrarium*, as it's called, is used for cleaning the chalice and paten used during communion. Any tiny crumbs of the consecrated Eucharist or small drops of the Precious Blood that remain after Mass will be washed down the sacrarium and returned to the earth in the most reverent disposal method we have. We believe this process is more suited to the revered vessels than just popping them in the dishwasher in the priest's house.

PART 3

Mass Prayers

16. How does the priest choose which Eucharistic Prayer to use?

17. How can I tell which Eucharistic Prayer the priest is using?

18. Why do some priests sing during Mass?

19. What are those "secret" prayers the priest whispers during Mass?

20. Are we supposed to say the Hail Mary as part of the Mass?

21. Why do we say, "I am not worthy to receive you," but then we do?

22. When we say, "Only say the word and my soul shall be healed"…what's the word?

16. How does the priest choose which Eucharistic Prayer to use?

As a lifelong Mass-goer, I've noticed that there are different Eucharistic Prayers that can be used, but I've always wondered how they are chosen for a specific Mass.

Vince in Coral Gables, Florida

Very perceptive! The various Eucharistic Prayers are found in the *Roman Missal*, the big book containing all the prayer texts and instructions we need to celebrate the Mass. First, I should probably quickly explain that the Eucharistic Prayer is the longest prayer in the Mass, used when blessing the bread and wine. We describe it as "the center and high point of the entire celebration" and as "the prayer of thanksgiving and sanctification" (*GIRM* 78). It begins after the altar has been prepared and gifts brought forward, and it ends with the Great Amen (often sung) just before we pray the Our Father.

The four main Eucharistic Prayers are simply titled Eucharistic Prayer I, Eucharistic Prayer II, and so on. There are also a few other optional Eucharistic Prayers that highlight themes such as reconciliation, serving the poor, and the unity of believers.

MASS PRAYERS

The most commonly used are numbers two and three. Eucharistic Prayer II is the shortest, and it is oftentimes chosen for its brevity, particularly during daily Mass. Although I will have to say, that distinction is somewhat artificial. I've timed it out: the actual difference between Eucharistic Prayers II and III is just about a minute.

It's really up to the priest who is celebrating Mass to choose which Eucharistic Prayer to use—and sometimes that decision is made on the spot, right at the altar. We are not mandated to use any particular Eucharistic Prayer, though some guidance is offered. For instance, number three is the only one of the four main Eucharistic Prayers that provides an opportunity for the priest to insert the name of the saint of the day into the prayer, so it would make sense to use number three on saint feast days. Eucharistic Prayer I is used less frequently, not only because it's longer. It has more in it, such as lists of saints and different actions and rituals that people aren't used to these days—more bowing and making the Sign of the Cross, for instance—and more pausing for silent prayer. Eucharistic Prayer IV is also a longer one that takes the form of a historical narrative, from creation through the Old Testament prophets and all the way up to Jesus's virgin birth and his ministry. It's a beautiful prayer, but oftentimes is not chosen because of its length and because you can't use a seasonal or feast-day preface with it.

I typically use Eucharistic Prayers II and III most often, but my favorite is Eucharistic Prayer for Reconciliation II. Part of it goes like this: "We humbly beseech you to accept us also, together with your Son, and in this saving banquet graciously to endow us with his very Spirit, who takes away everything that estranges us from one another. May he make your Church a sign of unity and an instrument of your peace among all people." I find that not infrequently something is going on in the Church or the world that makes that prayer very relevant and necessary!

17. How can I tell which Eucharistic Prayer the priest is using?

I like to follow along with the Mass, so how do I know which Eucharistic Prayer the priest will be using? I sometimes spend the first couple of minutes flipping through the pages in the missalette.

Camilla in Thousand Oaks, California

The best suggestion I have is that you play the odds. My very nonscientific data gathering reveals that about 80 percent of the time the priest will choose either Eucharistic Prayer II or III. So, keep your thumb on those two pages in the missalette. Then begin to listen after the Sanctus (Holy, Holy, Holy…). You won't be able to tell immediately because both of these follow the Sanctus with the words "You indeed are holy, O Lord…." But right after that they diverge. Eucharistic Prayer II picks up with "the fount of all holiness," whereas number three has "and all you have created rightly gives you praise." So, within a few seconds you can find the right one and be in sync with the priest.

One other pro tip: if you're at daily Mass, you can probably start with the page open to Eucharistic Prayer II as the odds are heavily in your favor there (unless it's a saint feast day, in which case, III might be more likely). Of course, these methods are not foolproof. In the *Roman Missal* there are ten different Eucharistic Prayers the priest can pick from, and there's really no good way to tell in advance which he's chosen.

But allow me to suggest something quite the opposite of what you're asking me. Let me challenge you to *not* follow along in the book but rather to simply join in the prayer of the Mass by listening to the words the priest prays. Take them in, internalize them. Let them wash over you. This also allows you to see what's going on and enjoy the beauty of your church. What we're doing at Mass is ritual. It is enacted, embodied prayer. It is most fully experienced not by reading along with a script but by making ourselves fully present to the prayers and actions of the Mass. Watch, listen, and respond, and you are participating as the Church intends. For example, there's a point in the Mass when the priest elevates the host and says, "Behold the Lamb of God," which in essence means, "Look up here at what we believe to be the True Presence of our Lord." Do you think the ideal is that when that happens you are glued to the page or you are in fact looking up at Christ present in our midst?

To use a more personal example: Imagine your first daughter getting married and you're in the front pew. Do you think your instinct at the moment of the exchange of vows (regardless of my advice) would be to look down to follow along with the exact words, or to lock your gaze on your daughter, and likely tear up?

If you really want to appreciate the particular words of the Eucharistic Prayers, try spending some time reading them over at home before Mass. That way, when the priest prays them aloud in church, they will sound familiar. In fact, if you've been going to Mass most of your life, you very likely know all the words already anyway! So give it a try: put down the book and see how your experience of praying the Mass changes.

18. Why do some priests sing during Mass?

I've noticed that some priests sing parts of the Mass and others don't. One priest at our parish sings the whole Mass! How is that decided?

Martha in Hudson, New York

First off, some priests are blessed with a great set of pipes, and some, well…aren't. Beyond that, some members of the clergy really value the ancient practice of chanting the Mass, while others, even though they are able to sing, still choose not to. Many priests I know will chant shorter parts of the Mass such as the "Mystery of Faith." But singing an entire Roman Catholic Mass is a practice that most experts would say should be reserved for special occasions. I say "Roman Catholic" because in the Eastern Catholic Rites and Orthodox churches, they chant or sing pretty much everything all the time.

You asked how it is decided. In our tradition, to sing or not to sing, and how much, is ultimately up to the discretion of the priest himself. Yet, there are some underlying principles of ritual celebration that should be considered here. One is the degree of solemnity, or level of importance, of the Mass (see *GIRM* 38). The Church believes there should be a noticeable difference between a Tuesday in Ordinary Time and Easter Sunday morning. For a special occasion, we "amp it up," by adding more flowers or more musicians, or using incense and finer chalices, and wearing finer vestments. Conversely, on a non-special occasion, the congregation should notice the lack of those things. Martha, if your husband put on a tuxedo for dinner at home every weeknight after work, that may seem a little odd, right? But if the two of you have reservations at fancy restaurant for New Year's Eve…much more appropriate.

mass class notes

Vestments:
outer garments
worn by ministers
during the celebration
of certain prayer
services (for more,
see question
35 in part 5)

Another principle at play here is that no single aspect of the Mass should draw so much attention to itself (or the priest to himself) that it distracts from the fundamental goal of worshiping God. In other words, when the people in the pews hear an entire Mass sung or chanted by the priest, they should be saying to themselves, "Today must be a really special day in the life of the Church," not, "I guess Father Joseph really likes singing the Mass." Priestly singing should be an informed decision based on universal norms, not merely a preference of the priest—no matter how great he sounds!

19. What are those "secret" prayers the priest whispers during Mass?

I try to pay attention closely at Mass, but there seem to be some prayers that the priest keeps secret from us. Why is that?

Fred in Oklahoma City, Oklahoma

You've got me wondering if you're a Latin scholar, Fred, because in the original Latin the instructions for a few prayers direct that they should be said *secreto*. But that doesn't mean they are a secret! The Italians translate this as *sotto voce*, or "in a soft voice." Our English *Roman Missal* uses the word "quietly." Both of these are faithful to the meaning of *secreto*. So honestly, the priest is not trying to hide something from you. The idea here is that while the vast majority of the prayers the priest prays during Mass are meant to lead the entire congregation (and thus should be audible to them), a few short prayers are not intended in that way.

These quiet prayers are ones the priest prays for himself, "asking that he may exercise his ministry with greater attention and devotion" (*GIRM* 33). Here are two examples. The first happens when the priest is about to proclaim the Gospel. He says in a soft voice, "Cleanse my heart and my lips, almighty God, that I may worthily proclaim your holy Gospel." And later, as he does a ritual hand washing during the preparation of the altar, he prays, "Lord, wash away my iniquity; cleanse me of my sin." As you can tell, these are moments when the priest personally expresses humility before God. I find these prayers to be very meaningful for me. They are reminders that it is indeed not my human abilities but rather the Holy Spirit using me as a vessel that allow the Mass to have an impact on those gathered for worship.

mass class notes

Roman Missal: big red book containing all the prayers the priest needs for Mass

Further, in the case of both of these *secreto* prayers, there would very likely be music or singing happening at the same time (at least on a Sunday), reinforcing the notion that these words are not necessary for the congregation to hear. So, Fred, don't worry. The priest is not being secretive; he's humbly seeking God's grace that he may be worthy to serve God's people in the celebration of the Mass.

20. Are we supposed to say the Hail Mary as part of the Mass?

My parish priest says the Hail Mary at every Mass after the General Intercessions. Isn't the Mass about Jesus and the Eucharist and aren't the intercessions the prayers of the faithful? Why do we bring Mary into it?

Sarah in Dennis, Massachusetts

The part of the Mass you're asking about has a few different names. Many of us continue to refer to it as the "General Intercessions" or the "Prayers of the Faithful." Technically it's now called the "Universal Prayer," and its basic structure is this: introduction by the priest; followed by the praying of several individual intentions (with an appropriate acclamation by the congregation, most often "Lord, hear our prayer"); and a concluding prayer said by the priest (see *GIRM* 71). Unlike other portions of the Mass, the Universal Prayer does not have a specific text prescribed for any of those three pieces, but only guidelines for the content. A certain latitude is granted with respect to this element of the Mass.

Sometimes the priest's introduction and concluding prayer are written out ahead of time, either by himself or a member of the parish staff. Then they're printed up, and the priest reads them like he would one of the prescribed prayers in the *Roman Missal*. Alternatively, both of these "bookends" to the intercessions may be uttered spontaneously by the priest.

One might argue that if we're crafting a prayer to round out all the intercessions, a suitable option might be to use a prayer we all know, one we can all join in together, like the Hail Mary. One parish might use the Glory Be; another a prayer to a particular saint, such as the patron saint of that parish; others might conclude with a stewardship prayer if there's a big fundraiser underway. Yours happens to conclude with the Hail Mary. Again, some latitude is allowed by the Church here.

While it's true that the "Mass is about Jesus and the Eucharist," as you put it, Sarah, we certainly do mention and honor the Blessed Mother during Mass, specifically in the Creed and again in the Eucharistic Prayer. Let me offer this one further connection as well. In the Hail Mary, we are asking for Mary's intercession ("pray for us sinners"). In the Universal Prayer, we are offering up several intercessions directly to God. Why not add the power of our Blessed Mother's intercessory prayer to our own? One final thought: your priest may find value in helping connect what we do at Mass with the everyday faith life of the congregation. There are very few other parts of the Mass that we would routinely pray on our own at home (the Lord's Prayer being the only other obvious example). Perhaps your priest is thinking, particularly with respect to children, that this simple practice at Sunday Mass might foster a greater Catholic devotion during the rest of the week.

21. Why do we say, "I am not worthy to receive you," but then we do?

I find it contradictory that we say aloud "Lord, I am not worthy to receive you," but then go right ahead and receive the Body and Blood of the Lord. Help me understand this.

Mel in Leesburg, Virginia

You're right, pretty much the last thing we do just before *receiving* communion is say, "Lord, I am not worthy that you should enter under my roof, but only say the word and my soul shall be healed" (and for many years, the English translation was as you remember it: "Lord, I'm not worthy to receive you...", the older version presenting an even greater apparent contradiction). And it would indeed be a bizarre, contradictory thing to say—*if* we stopped halfway through the sentence.

Let's think of it this way: Suppose you showed up at somebody's house with whom you'd had a fight that week. They open the door with a dubious look on their face. You say, "I don't deserve to be admitted to your party, but if you say the word, we—our relationship—will be healed." And that person cracks a smile, offers a hug, and lets you in. You would only bother to show up at the house if you at least had some small hope that your friend would put this all behind you and welcome you in.

That humble exchange illustrates the intent of the phrase from the Mass that you're asking about. Basically, we're admitting our unworthiness but also our confidence in God's mercy. Even as we get close to communion, we're saying, "Lord, I have to be honest, and say, 'I am a sinner.' And yet you want me to come forward. Your word of healing allows me to bask in your mercy and receive communion."

22. When we say, "Only say the word and my soul shall be healed"... what's the word?

Father Dave, here's something I've always wondered–and I hope it's not too weird a question. Before communion, we all say, "Lord, I'm not worthy that you should enter under my roof, but only say the word, and my soul shall be healed." What's the "word" we're referring to?

Ellie in Greensboro, North Carolina

No, it's not weird. In fact, this is a frequently asked question here on the show, so you are definitely not alone in wondering about this. The simple answer is that it's an idiom, a turn of phrase. Have you ever heard someone say something like, "I want to be there for you, so just *say the word* and I'll drop what I'm doing and come over"? What they mean is the other person doesn't need to describe their need or persuade them to come over—that is, they won't need to use a lot of words. Just one word will do, and it doesn't even matter which one.

Remember the film *Jerry Maguire* with Tom Cruise? In the classic scene after Jerry bursts in on Renée Zellweger's character, Dorothy, and gives a fairly lengthy, tearful apology, there's a moment of dramatic tension before she responds, "You had me at 'hello.'" Turns out, he didn't need that long, rehearsed speech after all. All he needed was one word.

Here's one more: Picture a navy captain inspecting his crew all standing at attention on the deck of the ship. The second-in-command informs him, "Ready to embark, sir. Just give the word and we'll shove off."

Apparently, this turn of phrase was also in use in Jesus's time (not in English, of course). In fact, the words for this part of the Mass are taken almost verbatim from an account in the Gospels (see Matthew 8:5–13 and Luke 7:1–10). A Roman centurion, a military commander, approaches Jesus and tells him of his dying servant back at his house several miles away. When Jesus offers to follow him all the way home so that he may heal his servant, the centurion says in reply, "Lord, I am not worthy to have you enter under my roof; only say the word and my servant will be healed." Does that sound familiar? It should. Substitute the word "servant" for the word "soul" and you've got that phrase from the Mass that befuddles you.

What the centurion means is essentially, "No, no, no. I'm not worthy that you, someone with such great power, would come all the way to my house. But I have faith in you. I believe that all you would need to do is say a single word from this far off and my servant will be healed right away." You'll notice that Jesus does not then say some sort of magic word like *abracadabra*. Why? Because "just say the word" doesn't mean there is a particular word that must be said. Rather, Jesus turns to the crowd and starts extolling the commander's great faith. Then the Lord proclaims, "You may go; as you have believed, let it be done for you." And the Scripture tells us that at that moment the servant was healed.

How fitting is it that just before we receive communion at Mass, we repeat the words of the centurion? It's a testament of our faith, just like it was for him. We, too, believe that, as sinful as we are, Christ has the power to heal us, to make us worthy. Maybe now, when you pray, "Lord, I am not worthy that you should enter under my roof, but only say the word and my soul shall be healed," you can hear in your heart our Lord saying to you, "As you have believed, let it be done for you."

PART 4

Receiving Communion

23. How many times can you receive the Eucharist in one day?

24. Does consuming two hosts count as receiving communion twice?

25. Can I receive communion if I asked for God's forgiveness during Mass?

26. Why can't my non-Catholic husband receive communion at Mass?

27. If someone only receives one communion element, which one is more important?

28. We can't catch germs by drinking the Blood of Christ, right?

29. Will they ever bring back the paten?

30. If the Eucharist accidentally drops on the floor, what should be done?

31. What is the best technique to receive communion on my tongue?

32. Why do we say "amen" when receiving communion?

33. How do you pronounce *amen*?

34. When do we go from kneeling to sitting after communion?

23. How many times can you receive the Eucharist in a day?

I'm a eucharistic minister and recently something came up. I served at the Sunday 8:00 a.m. Mass as scheduled. When I got home, one of the 11:00 a.m. Mass ministers called and said, "I can't make Mass this morning. Can you cover for me? You're my last hope, I've asked three people already!" I said sure. But when I arrived at church, it dawned on me: "I've already had communion today! Am I allowed to receive again at this Mass?" Are there rules on how many times Catholics can receive communion in one day?

Tom in Milpitas, California

I'm curious to know what you decided, Tom, but I won't put you on the spot. You asked if there are rules regarding this. I hope it doesn't surprise you to find out that there are. In fact, when anyone asks me a question that contains the words "Are there rules?," there's a high likelihood that my answer is going to be yes. And I won't keep you in suspense much longer: there is nothing wrong with you receiving communion twice on that Sunday that you pitched in to help. So don't worry; you're fine.

Normally, a Catholic would not receive communion more than once a day, meaning they wouldn't attend multiple Masses, except on some occasions when it is appropriate. An example is if someone who regularly attends the 7:30 a.m. daily Mass at their parish also went to a funeral Mass in the afternoon. That person should have no concerns about receiving communion a second time.

The *Code of Canon Law* (a big fat book that contains lots of the aforementioned "rules") prescribes that "a person who has received the Most Holy Eucharist may receive it again on the same day only during the celebration of the Eucharist in which the person participates" (canon 917). There are a few things to note in that short statement.

First, the law allows you to max out at two. Even a busy deacon who ends up serving at three Masses on the same day technically should abstain from receiving communion at the third Mass. Two is the limit unless you are dying (canon law is filled with exemptions for those who are close to death). The next thing that's interesting is that this regulation does not require that receiving communion twice in a day be only on rare occasions for some "grave reason." In other words, you would not have had to submit a letter to your bishop defending your action at that 11:00 a.m. Mass, complete with testimony from the other minister citing how many other calls she made. In fact, the implication here is if my Aunt Angie really wants to receive the Eucharist at daily Mass in the morning before she goes to work *and* in the evening on her way home, she is permitted to do that.

Finally, the most curious wording of canon 917 is actually the reason why the law exists in the first place. You may have thought it odd for the Church to include the phrase "only during the celebration of the Eucharist in which the person participates." Well, duh? How could you even receive communion at a Mass you're not participating in? This law is attempting to guard against the temptation to think we can "multiply the grace" of the sacrament by receiving communion more frequently. It's not inconceivable that a person could figure out when different Mass times are around town, and just pop into the church during the communion procession, join the line, receive the Eucharist, and then head on over to the parish with the next Mass and repeat the process. The Church does not want us to get the idea that the Blessed Sacrament is some sort of elixir: the more of it we consume over the course of a day, the more healing it brings. Not so. That's why the law stipulates that someone must "participate in the Mass" at which they receive.

The Eucharist is not a fast-food drive through window. Rather it's more akin to a family's Thanksgiving dinner. You show up early, hang around a while gathered at the table, hear family stories, eat plenty of food, and leave when everyone else does—when it's all over. So canon 917 is saying, "If you wanna do that twice in one day, be our guest. But don't think you can just drop in for pumpkin pie and take it on a paper plate to go."

Again, in your case, as an extraordinary minister of Holy Communion serving at two different Masses on a Sunday, receiving communion a second time is acceptable in the Church's eyes because you fully participated in both Masses.

24. Does consuming two hosts count as receiving communion twice?

Father Dave, I have a follow-up to that last question. Does consuming more than one host at a time count as receiving communion again?

Kendra in Newark, Delaware

Actually, I'm glad you asked that because I've got a fun story (embarrassing for me) that can illustrate the answer. I'll begin by saying this is most apropos for someone who is an extraordinary minister of Holy Communion. It is not unheard of that a priest or lay minister might need to consume some extra hosts at the end of the communion rite in certain situations, namely when a tabernacle is not available in the vicinity. This might happen at a Catholic conference or convention when Mass is celebrated in a nonchurch venue like a hotel ballroom, or even at some special parish Mass outside in a park. The answer to your question is no: if you are given three or four hosts to consume, it does not constitute "receiving communion" three or four times, and thus you're not violating any Church rules. But the problem is that most people are unfamiliar with this because it comes up so rarely.

Does consuming two hosts count as communion twice?

And here I speak from experience. I have on occasion served as the Catholic chaplain on a cruise ship (pretty sweet gig, by the way). Most times we end up having our Mass in a meeting room on a folding table, often with the ship rocking from side to side. But more germane to this discussion, there is no tabernacle onboard. So I try my best to estimate the exact number of hosts we will need for communion, so as not to consecrate too few or too many. But I don't always get the count spot-on. One time I noticed toward the end of the communion procession that there were going to be quite a few consecrated hosts left over. In my head, I had to make the snap decision: I could either stick around after Mass and consume a whole bunch of hosts, or I could give two or three hosts each to the last few people in line. I chose the latter. That's a mistake I won't make again. The people in line were looking at me as if I just placed gummy bears in their hands instead of the Body of Christ—just because I gave them more than one host! It is unusual and most people don't expect it. And for that reason, since then I've consumed all the extra hosts myself.

25. Can I receive communion if I asked for God's forgiveness during Mass?

I was always told we need to go to confession before receiving communion, but I notice that at the beginning of Mass we call to mind our sins and ask for forgiveness—doesn't that count?

Leonard in Rapid City, South Dakota

You're right that we specifically ask for God's mercy and forgiveness several times during Mass prior to communion. The first occurs in a part of the Mass called the Penitential Act. This happens pretty much right after we make the Sign of the Cross at the very beginning, and most often includes our saying, "Lord have mercy, Christ have mercy, Lord have mercy." One of the optional forms even uses the words, "I confess to almighty God and to you, my brothers and sisters, that I have greatly sinned." The priest follows this up with the prayer, "May almighty God have mercy on us, forgive us our sins, and bring us to everlasting life." Well, that sure sounds as though all is taken care of. But there's an important distinction to be made here: between venial sins and mortal sins.

Venial sins are the everyday ways that we believers "miss the mark" (the literal meaning of the word *sin*) and do not live up to our calling as followers of Christ. These are selfish actions, immoral choices, harmful words, lustful thoughts, and so on. Mortal sins are much more severe. They are so damaging that they actually cut us off from God and the Christian community; they break off our communion with the Church. During the course of the Mass, our venial sins are forgiven (see *CCC* 1394), but "the Eucharist is not ordered to the forgiveness of mortal sins—that is proper to the sacrament of Reconciliation. The Eucharist is properly the sacrament of those who are in full communion with the Church" (*CCC* 1395).

This is what we mean when we say one needs to go to confession before receiving communion. We are obligated to confess those *grave sins* that have taken us "out of communion" with God and one another and be absolved of those sins thus returning us to "full communion" with the Church. Ideally, we Catholics should periodically examine our conscience with the aid of the Holy Spirit, since that is how we discern whether or not we have committed a mortal sin. If we determine we have, then we should avail ourselves of the sacrament of reconciliation (or, as we say, "go to confession") at some point before going to Mass so that we will be able to receive communion (see *CCC* 1457). If we haven't had a chance to do that, and we get to that point in the Mass when the priest invites us to "call to mind our sins," and all of a sudden what comes to mind is a mortal sin, then we should abstain from receiving communion at that Mass and get ourselves to the confessional sometime soon!

26. Why can't my non-Catholic husband receive communion at Mass?

My husband was raised Lutheran, but ever since we were married, he attends Catholic Mass with me on Sundays. He feels left out at communion time. Why is he not allowed to take the Eucharist?

Betty in St. Cloud, Minnesota

First, let me say that I can imagine how difficult this must be for him, and also for you. No one likes feeling excluded, nor feeling like they are part of the group doing the excluding, particularly of a loved one. So I'm sorry about that. Here's where the Catholic Church is coming from on this.

The most pertinent answer to your question is found in the word *communion*. It means "in union with." We believe that sacramentally receiving communion symbolizes a union that exists between God and the individual communicant, while also further deepening that union. But it also symbolizes a unity that exists among all people receiving communion, and similarly further strengthens that bond of unity.

The reality is that the Lutheran Church and the Catholic Church are not fully in union with one another (and this of course would apply to a host of other Christian churches as well). Because a common union does not exist, the act of receiving sacramental communion can neither symbolize unity nor strengthen a nonexistent union.

mass class notes

Communicant: churchy term for the person receiving communion

Even though we live in a modern world where many people dismiss the differences between Christian denominations or claim something akin to "all roads lead to the top of the mountain," the truth is the Body of Christ on earth remains divided. Our *Catechism of the Catholic Church* teaches,

> Ecclesial communities derived from the Reformation and separated from the Catholic Church, "have not preserved the proper reality of the Eucharistic mystery in its fullness, especially because of the absence of the sacrament of Holy Orders." It is for this reason that, for the Catholic Church, Eucharistic intercommunion with these communities is not possible. (*CCC* 1400)

Now, I can just imagine your husband responding, "But I wasn't there in the sixteenth century when Martin Luther decided to break communion with the Church. It's not my fault there is disunity between Catholics and Lutherans, so why am I seemingly being punished?" That's a fair question. Think of a slightly different scenario where your husband had married someone who's a citizen of another country and the couple decided to live in that country for a few years after getting married. He likely would feel he was being treated differently than his wife in her native land, even excluded from certain things. There may be a language barrier (which is awkward and makes one feel left out), or depending on the country, he may not be able to get a driver's license or have access to healthcare or other services. But it's also quite possible there would be a path available to him toward full citizenship that would solve most of those issues of exclusion.

And that is also the case with the Catholic Church. If your husband desires to receive communion along with everyone else, we welcome him to begin a process to enter into full communion with the Church called the RCIA (Rite of Christian Initiation of Adults). I know many non-Catholic spouses who have really appreciated going through this process of prayer and education and are happy they now share a common religious experience with their spouse. Your husband may not be inclined to convert to Catholicism for any number of reasons. That's understandable. But in that case, just like living in a foreign country and not wanting to pursue citizenship, there will still be one or two things not fully available to him in the Catholic Church, notably, receiving communion. But it really is up to him.

27. If someone only receives one communion element, which one is more important?

I've noticed that some people receive the host but do not drink from the chalice, but some people do the opposite. First of all, do we have to consume both elements? Is it an insult to receive one and not the other? Or is it improper because it's an incomplete ritual?

Stephen on Long Island, New York

In the beginnings of Christianity, everybody received Holy Communion "under both species" or "under both kinds," that is, both the consecrated bread and the consecrated wine, the Body and Blood of Jesus. Over the centuries, however, there have been long stretches of time when the congregation was only given the host; the priest was the only one to receive from the chalice. Often this was done for health reasons, for instance, during the Middle Ages because of the plague, and more recently during the COVID-19 global pandemic. So clearly, we are not required to receive both.

The ritual is not incomplete or improper if someone only receives one and not the other (see *CCC* 1390).

But is a person getting cheated out of some grace by only receiving one of the two species? No. Theologically, the Church relies on the principle of *concomitance*: because Christ is indivisible, Christ is fully present—body, blood, soul, and divinity—in both the consecrated bread and the consecrated wine. This means that Christ's body and blood are *both* fully present in merely the consecrated host, as they are also in the consecrated wine (see *CCC* 1377). If that were not true, we'd all be in trouble because Jesus warns in chapter 6 of John's Gospel, "Unless you eat the flesh of the Son of Man and drink his blood, you do not have life within you" (John 6:53). He says we gotta do both! The principle of concomitance assures us that we have done both, even when we only receive one of the two elements. And although the communion minister does only say "the Body of Christ" when offering you the host, and "the Blood of Christ" when offering you the chalice, let me reiterate: Christ's *body, blood, soul, and divinity* are fully present in each of the species.

So, you don't get any more Jesus by receiving under both kinds. You don't get more grace. It's not better. And it's certainly not sinful if you don't receive both. It's completely up to the communicant (the person receiving communion) to choose if they want to receive under both kinds—that is, if both kinds are being offered at the Mass you're attending.

You also asked if it's an insult. While I could not speak to whether or not a priest or other communion minister might give you a strange look based on your choice—ideally, they should not. I can confidently tell you that Jesus is not insulted if you choose not to receive from the chalice. The same is true of those who choose to receive *only* from the chalice. For example, members of the faithful who have celiac disease or a gluten sensitivity will often choose not to consume the wheat-based host since doing so may cause serious medical problems for them. Hopefully, an increasing awareness of and sensitivity to issues like this result in fewer side-eye looks from those distributing communion.

Because neither communion element is more important than the other, you can choose either or both. It's all the same to God, and you're getting the same amount of grace. Let's not forget: Jesus is the Lord of the universe; if he wants to permeate our body and soul, he's going to do that whether it's through a liquid or solid form. The Holy Eucharist is the source and summit of our faith, no matter how we receive it.

28. We can't catch germs by drinking the Blood of Christ, right?

After a recent medical procedure, my doctor advised me not to drink from the chalice at Mass because I am now immunocompromised. But my mother said that I cannot get sick because we believe it is no longer wine but the pure blood of Christ and there can be no germs in Christ's Precious Blood. Who should I listen to?

Tina in Silver Spring, Maryland

Boy, am I glad you asked! Let me tell you in no uncertain terms to listen to your doctor, not your mother (on this matter, anyway). First of all, human blood can in fact carry disease, maybe even more easily than wine can, so merely saying "it's blood not wine" doesn't get you anywhere. Nor do we believe that the Precious Blood of Christ is some magical blood that repels germs or heals injuries like the water poured from the Holy Grail chalice onto Sean Connery's bullet wound in the climatic scene of *Indiana Jones and the Last Crusade*. That's fiction, not our religious belief.

The change in the elements of bread and wine that occurs during the Eucharistic Prayer is not a transformation but a "transubstantiation." One might think we can use those words interchangeably. Not true. The distinction is crucial—particularly in your case when it could make a life-or-death difference! A *trans-form*-ation is a change in the form (the "outside") of something. Tran-*substanti*-ation means a change in the substance or essence (the "inside") of a thing. The teaching of the Catholic Church is that after being consecrated by the priest during Mass, the *substance* of what was simply bread and wine is now the True Presence of Christ's Body and Blood, *under the appearance* of bread and wine. And the word *appearance* here means more than just what they look like; it refers to any way in which we can humanly perceive or measure the material aspects of the elements (see *CCC* 1381). For instance, the alcohol content, color, and taste of the wine remain. Therefore, its potential to carry germs also remains, and someone with a medical condition could still be seriously affected.

Yes, we believe that this is truly the Blood of Christ, but that doesn't mean we believe that what's in the chalice at communion time should have the consistency or molecular makeup of human blood. Nope, it still has all the characteristics of cheap table wine, and it is not somehow made magically impervious to germs. The same can be said of the host. People with celiac disease, who could very possibly have a life-threatening reaction to ingesting even a small amount of wheat, know quite well that the host has the same gluten content before and after the consecration. No doubt, your mom's faith and devotion to the Eucharist are to be commended. But it's always important to *understand* what we believe.

29. Will they ever bring back the paten?

Father, could the paten ever make a comeback, you know, so the host won't drop on the floor? I know it would take more eucharistic ministers or altar servers to help.

Monica in Palm Beach, Florida

For those who need to brush up on Mass vocabulary, a paten is a small, shallow plate, typically made of gold or silver, that can serve two purposes. The first is to contain hosts on the altar and act as a "serving plate" during the distribution of communion. The second use, and I believe the one you're asking about, Monica, is to prevent the host from hitting the floor while communion is being distributed. This type of paten typically has a handle attached so that an altar server may stick it right under the chin of someone about to receive the host. The first type of paten I still use every time I celebrate Mass, so it hasn't gone anywhere. Will the handle type make a comeback? I doubt it. Here's why.

When Mass was celebrated prior to 1970, the faithful would kneel along an altar rail to receive the Eucharist on the tongue from the priest who would move across the railing. With this practice, there often would be an altar boy accompanying him maneuvering a paten under the chin of the communicant so that just in case the host were to miss the tongue, it would fall onto the nice little metal plate instead of dropping to the floor. While some altar boys had steadier hands than others, this approach had a fair probability of success in that situation—one where there's an altar rail and the communicant is firmly planted, kneeling, and their chin and head are not moving that much. Today, following the changes to the Mass called for by the Second Vatican Council (1962–65), most communion processions are different. As you know, instead of people kneeling in place and the priest moving around, now it is the priest or communion minister who stands still while the communicants line up and process toward them. In my experience, there's a fairly continuous movement of the line. Often people don't even come to a full halt when they're receiving communion. They just kind of slow down—like a slow roll through a stop sign— which makes it much more difficult to hold something under their chin and catch a potentially falling host. So it's not really practical to use a paten in that way today.

If you ever watched Cirque du Soleil performers tossing one another in the air, you've perhaps had that nervous feeling in your stomach as you wonder, "Is he gonna catch her!?" Yet, I'd give those gymnasts much higher odds of a catch than an altar server attempting to intercept a rogue falling host at Mass today.

There's another dimension to this that goes beyond mere logistics. Clearly, a profound reverence is appropriate when receiving the Body of Christ. After all, we believe it really is Jesus himself we are taking into our very bodies! This means that those distributing communion and those receiving it have a duty to safeguard this reverence with our actions, as well as with our attitudes. In simpler terms, we should all take great care when handling and consuming the Eucharist. In my assessment, though, in years past, this healthy deference morphed into an overly cautious, even paranoid approach to communion—as if a host inadvertently dropping to the floor would cause the earth to open up and swallow all those in a hundred-foot radius. I believe in the decades since the reform of the Mass most of us have adopted a more balanced approach to reverence during communion. It might be something akin to this: Let's be as reverent and careful and intentional as possible, but we are all human and accidents happen. Think about it: In Jesus's thirty-three years on earth, do you think he ever stumbled and fell down? Was he surrounded by two big security guards 24/7 to make sure that if he tripped on a rock he would not fall to the ground? Of course not. Our Lord can take it, and furthermore he's not mad at us when there's a communion mishap, so we can stand to be less fearful as we come forth to receive him.

Now, just in case you think me too glib or not respectful enough of Christ's True Presence in the sacrament because of what I just said, allow me to conclude by challenging all of us—myself included—to step up our reverence game at Mass. Things we do with great repetition can sometimes become monotonous or rushed. Remember my analogy of rolling through a stop sign? I encourage you to not rush through your reception of communion. Consider it like the full stop you'd make in your car if you knew a police officer was watching that intersection. It is something incredibly profound that we are participating in. Let's treat it that way. (But also, don't flip out if the host drops!)

30. If the Eucharist accidentally drops on the floor, what should be done?

Last week, something terrible happened to me for the first time: when I went up to receive communion, the host accidentally dropped to the floor. I was mortified! What should I have done?

Burt in Henderson, Nevada

This does rarely happen, but let me underscore one word in your question: *accidentally*. As careful and as reverent as we are, accidents do happen, and God is not mad. If you're a parent, for instance, you may remember the first time your child got a cut or scrape or bruise while playing. Tears! Screaming! Wailing! To them, because they had never experienced it before, it was like the end of the world. You as the wizened parent, however—while smiling, hugging, and consoling—knew it was really no big deal. Given this was your first experience with what we here at Busted Halo call a "Mass Hap," I can't tell you that you should not have felt mortified. But please know that God, our Heavenly Parent, was giving you the same consoling hug on Sunday. Okay, but onto your question: "What should be done?"

There's two people involved in this exchange: you, the communicant, and the minister (priest, deacon, or extraordinary minister of Holy Communion). It is my firm opinion that in the case of a dropped host, the communicant should do nothing. Just stand still for a moment. I know it's counterintuitive because you can't help but want to react to something like that. Please try. Almost assuredly, you both know what just happened. Allow the person who is trained, practiced, and spirituality formed for this moment to deal with it. They will pick it up off the floor and one of a few things might happen next.

They may quickly consume the host themselves; they may hold onto it separately from the rest of the hosts to do something with it later; they may walk away so they can put the host somewhere else to be dealt with later (in some cases, the host might be left to dissolve over time in holy water); or…they may just try to offer you that same host again, the one they just picked up off the floor. That last option would be rare, I think, but not unimaginable. The most likely scenario is that the minister picks it up and gives you a new host right away, which you then consume as usual and return to the pew trying hard not to blame yourself (God doesn't). Again, I encourage you to not react quickly, if for no other reason than to avoid the inevitable head collision if you both bend down quickly to grab the dropped host.

However, let's say for the sake of argument that for some reason the communion minister does not notice that the host dropped. In that case, you as the communicant have two options: you can point it out to the minister, who will then take one of the courses of action I just mentioned, or you can pick the host up off the floor and consume it yourself. Some people might be worried that doing that is somehow sacrilegious, or that the host is "desecrated" by hitting the floor. Neither are true. More folks might have a justified concern about germs. Five-second rule? If you're not comfortable eating something off the church floor, simply make the communion minister aware of what happened.

Whatever you do, please do not either leave it there on the floor and walk away, nor pick it up and bring it back to your seat, hoping to deal with it after Mass. Consume it as soon as you pick it up.

Remember, God is not mad when the host drops. He likely has more reason to be angry with us when we overlook the poor, post mean-spirited things on the internet, or withhold forgiveness from someone who has harmed us. Yet, even in those cases, God offers us mercy.

31. What is the best technique to receive communion on my tongue?

I just became a Catholic recently and I chose to receive the Eucharist on my tongue...but I think I'm doing something wrong, because the priest often ends up touching my lips or my tongue. And one time I thought I was going to bite his finger off. Is there some kind of secret Catholic technique I should learn?

Felicia in Chase City, Virginia

First of all, Felicia, welcome to the family! Glad you're with us. You said you've made the choice to receive communion on your tongue, a choice the Church offers each of us in its official directives: "The communicant receives the Sacrament either on the tongue or, where this is allowed and, if the communicant so chooses, in the hand" (*GIRM* 161). You may notice that it says, "where this is allowed." For many centuries, the only option for receiving communion was on the tongue and that is still considered the universal norm of the Catholic Church. But in the late 1960s, the even more ancient practice of receiving in the hand was also added as an option, but only granted to particular countries upon request of their bishops. Since then, that list has grown to the point where it would be uncommon not to be given the choice of receiving either on the tongue or in the hand wherever you are in the world.

Of course we always try to be as reverent as possible in the distribution of communion, so forgive me if our discussion begins to sound disrespectful to our Lord's presence in the Eucharist—but what you're asking has to do with very practical, human, bodily matters, so here it goes.

If occasionally the priest makes contact with your tongue or lips, it doesn't necessarily mean you're doing something wrong. But I can offer some pro tips that might

mass class notes

GIRM: *The General Instruction of the Roman Missal,* which tells us what to do and what not to do when celebrating Catholic Mass, and why

reduce the frequency of this from my perspective as someone who distributes communion. The best advice I can give are the words you may also hear from your doctor: "Open wide and stick out your tongue."

Some people probably feel that if they extend their tongue it's being disrespectful—as if childishly sticking out their tongue at Jesus or the priest. But you're actually doing us a favor. As a priest, I'm not insulted by seeing more of your tongue. And Jesus is not offended if you stick your tongue way out. If you don't, we communion ministers will end up playing a version of that old board game Operation, where the game buzzes and you lose points for touching the sides. The smaller the opening you give me with your tongue all hidden inside, the more likely I am to hear the buzzer sound on the game. (Again, I'm drawing this analogy to make a practical point, not to equate the True Presence of Christ with a children's board game.)

While some barely open their lips, others try to grab the Eucharist, either with their teeth or their lips. Please don't do that. Always remember that during communion we are *receiving* the Lord, not taking him, grabbing him, or snatching him. Our posture is to be open and receptive just like our hearts are to be.

One last thing: You might be concerned about the host falling off your tongue if it is extended too far out. My experience is that almost all of the hosts we use will actually stick to your tongue, so in practice that's a nonissue. And I know this is not your choice, but as long as we're on the topic, if you'll indulge me, I'll give a couple of tips for those receiving in the hand.

We can identify sources as far back as the third century that describe the practice of communion in the hand like this: "In approaching therefore, come not with your wrists extended, or your fingers spread; but make your left hand a throne for the right, as for that which is to receive a king." Simply place one hand under the other with a slight curvature to form a cup (you may choose either hand, despite the ancient world's bias toward right-handed people). I've seen some people put their two hands together, joined at the pinkie fingers. The problem there is that this is more like a trap door; if the host lands in the middle of that, you can't remove one hand to receive it, without the host falling out of the bottom! If one hand is under the other, making a throne for Christ, then when the host is placed in the top hand, the bottom hand may come around and pick it up.

Once more let me warn against the temptation to *grab*. We *receive* Christ as a gift, something we could not earn on our own merit. We're not walking to the kitchen cupboard and plucking out some snack we think we deserve. Rather, we're coming humbly and opening ourselves, either our mouths or our hands, and allowing Christ to be placed there.

32. Why do we say "amen" when receiving communion?

I have always dutifully said "amen" before receiving communion, but I've often wondered, what does it actually mean?

Carmen in Corpus Christi, Texas

Amen is an ancient word that is difficult to precisely translate, which is why we leave it in its original form rather than attempting to render it in modern languages. Its origins in Hebrew are associated with a person affirming or upholding some sort of testimony. We might say *corroborating* in a courtroom today. Or a guy on a street corner in Brooklyn might agree with his buddy by exclaiming, "Yeah, what *he* said!"

Down through the centuries, "amen" has been used by people in religious contexts to confirm or voice approval of something that has been proclaimed or prayed by someone else. In Paul's first letter to the Corinthians we see one of the earliest examples of the word being used in this way (1 Corinthians 14:16). The *Catechism of the Catholic Church*, quoting St. Cyril of Jerusalem from the fourth century, instructs us, "After the prayer is over you say 'amen,' which means 'So be it,' thus ratifying with our 'amen' what is contained in the prayer that God has taught us" (*CCC* 2856). So most generically, when we respond "amen" during Mass, we are essentially saying "yes, I agree."

In the communion rite, however, there are additional layers of meaning. I remember learning a new term during my time in seminary: *multivalent*. It refers to a prayer, ritual action, or even a single word that can contain multiple meanings, values, or uses all at the same time. Saying "amen" just before we receive communion is one such instance of multivalence. Let's look at three traditional meanings of our Eucharistic "amen."

mass class notes

Communion Rite: the part of the Mass where the people come forward to receive communion

The first is perhaps the most obvious: When the communion minister shows you the consecrated host and says the words, "The Body of Christ," it may very well seem as though he or she is asking for your assent of faith. "Do you, Carmen, indeed believe that this is truly the presence of our Lord Jesus Christ, body, blood, soul, and divinity?" Your response could be loosely translated, "Yes, I believe. I affirm that it's not just a wafer, but it is the body of my Lord." Your "amen" affirms your belief in the True Presence. But it does so much more than that.

Doctor of the Church St. Augustine preached a sermon about the Eucharist seventeen hundred years ago that still hits the mark today. He reminded us, "You are saying 'amen' to what you are: your response is a personal signature, affirming your faith. When you hear 'The body of Christ,' you reply 'amen.' Be a member of Christ's body, then, so that your "amen" may ring true....Be what you see; receive what you are" (Sermon 272). It might elude us at times that the phrase *the Body of Christ*—the very words spoken as the host is held up—refers not only to that piece of consecrated bread but also to *us* as Christians. We are the Body of Christ! For Augustine, our "amen" response is not limited to "yes, it is," but also encompasses "yes, we are."

The third meaning is my personal favorite but also may be the most challenging. The sacrament gives us God's grace. But God does not force this unmerited gift of love down our throat; it is a generous offer with which we must choose to cooperate. Receiving communion is not like drinking a magic potion that turns us into better, more loving, more merciful, or more charitable people for a few days until its effects wear off. To receive the very essence of our Lord within our bodies carries with it the responsibility to live a life commensurate with that gift; to make right choices, to make sacrifices, to think less of me and more of others, to forgive, to make peace, to love. The miraculous change on the altar from bread and wine to body and blood is not the only change the Mass is meant to bring about. We too must allow ourselves to be changed by this Eucharist. So, imagine the communion minister showing you the host and asking, "Do you agree to allow the presence of Christ to transform your life this week?" I bet you might take a little pause and even feel a lump in your throat before giving your "amen" to that.

Yes, it is. Yes, we are. Yes, I will. That's what you mean when you say "amen" before receiving communion. Pretty powerful word, isn't it?

33. How do you pronounce *amen?*

It surprises me the number of people during Mass that will say "ay-men" as opposed to "ah-men." Is there a correct way to pronounce it?

Lydia in El Dorado, Arkansas

Interesting question! As a priest, I hear the most "amens" when giving out communion. I would say that in my experience, not only at the parish where I serve but also in my travels across the United States, the "ay-men" spoken pronunciation is considerably more popular. I say "spoken" because when the word comes up in a hymn or chant, the scales tip the other way. It's far more common for Catholics to *sing* amen with an "ah" sound. That doesn't mean the "ah" is better or more appropriate at Mass; it probably just sounds better when sung with particular religious music. On the other hand, if you're in the stands at a football game trying to intimidate the opposing team, you may choose to go with one of the few sung instances of "ay-men," complete with hand swaying—but I digress.

Aside from how "ah-men" holds sway musically, I'm sure there are some Catholics who feel it's a little more "high church" or more traditional or perhaps even more reverent if you say "ah-men" rather than "ay-men." To that, I say fiddlesticks. Like any word, pronunciation may vary based on your language or cultural upbringing. If you're an English-speaking American living in the Texas panhandle, you'll likely pronounce "amen" differently than would the British prime minister. Case in point, albeit from a non-Catholic worship experience: just picture a classic African American Protestant preacher dabbing his brow mid-sermon and riling up his congregation with, "Can I get an ayyy—men?!" Once we start associating reverence in worship with a particular vowel sound, it's time to take a step back and appreciate the diversity of the Body of Christ.

I can confidently say that there is no official teaching about the spoken pronunciation of the word "amen." So let's not fret over how to pronounce it, but rather focus on the important part: *what* we are saying. *Amen* means "I believe" or "truly" or "so be it." However you pronounce it, just make sure you mean it!

34. When do we go from kneeling to sitting after communion?

I hope you can help me with something. After I receive communion, I return to the pew and kneel down to pray. So does most everyone else. My question is, at what point is it okay for me to sit back in the pew? I notice other people seem to be waiting for a particular cue from the priest. What should I be looking for?

Theresa in Aurora, Colorado

This is a very popular question, one that I'm afraid will probably not have as clear an answer as you would like. In my experience, I have observed generally three different points at which people change their posture from kneeling to sitting following communion. They are (1) when the priest sits down in his chair; (2) when the tabernacle door is shut; (3) or simply when an individual has finished praying his or her personal prayers. In some parishes you'll notice the great majority of the people in the pews exercising either the first or second option pretty much in unison. I've also been at some Masses where the congregation practices a mixture of all three of these, resulting in people moving to the sitting position at different times over the course of a few minutes.

There's even one last variant that stems from far more practical and human considerations than spiritual or theological ones. If the person in the pew directly in front of you sits back, you often have no choice but to do the same lest you end up poking them in the back with your folded praying hands. It's kind of like when a middle-aged person like me attends a concert. When the band first comes out on stage, the initial excitement will often lead to the whole crowd standing up. At some point (maybe after the second song?), there seems to be a growing consensus that it's time to sit down—after all, we're not teenagers anymore! But if the people in the back sit down before those in the front, they can't see. So the whole place tends to wait until some in the front begin to sit. Then you see a large wave of sitting washing over the concert venue, from front to back. I've seen something resembling this in churches after communion, seemingly motivated by nothing more than the people in the front pews feeling it was time to sit back.

Why is there so much variety on this from parish to parish, or even at the very same Mass? What's the "right" answer from Church teaching as to when we may sit back? The issue is, there is not one clear answer. The *General Instruction of the Roman Missal* says merely, "If appropriate, (the faithful) may *sit or kneel* while the period of sacred silence after Communion is observed," and that the purpose of this quiet time is for us "to praise God in [our] hearts and pray to him" (*GIRM* 43, 45; emphasis added). As for the priest, the *Order of Mass* directs that after communion he "may" return to the chair (138), implying that he also legitimately might not. Boy, that's an awful lot of ambiguity. When we read terms like "if appropriate" and "may," and encounter an "or" between two different postures, we can be assured the Church is trying hard for us to understand that there is not only one universally correct thing to be doing at this point in the Mass.

This in no way is meant to signal that the Church regards what happens after communion to be unimportant. Rather, the latitude in the instructions allows for an appropriate application of local custom or even for adjusting to particular circumstances. So the "cues" for sitting may vary from place to place, and that's okay. If you're at a Mass where a great majority of people wait until the Eucharist is returned to the tabernacle, then go ahead and wait until you see (or hear) that metal door slam shut. Sometimes the presiding priest will model this behavior by remaining standing and facing the tabernacle while some other minister places the consecrated hosts inside; then he will sit together with the whole congregation. In other parishes, the priest may sit down in his chair well before this moment, as others go about cleaning up after communion. Many people will likely take their cue from him, which is appropriate as this could rightly be interpreted as the presider giving a kind of nonverbal direction (see *GIRM* 43). So when it comes to this practice, the answer is essentially, "Check your local listings." Watch what other people do.

Finally, as with many things in the Christian life, I'd encourage you to err on the side of acting in an other-centered manner, not a self-centered one. For instance, in the absence of any kind of uniform cue, if the person behind you wants to remain on their knees for a little longer than would be your preference, rather than sitting back and crowding them, stay kneeling and give them their space.

PART 5

The Priest and Ministers

35. Why does the priest wear special ornate clothing during Mass?

36. Is there something that dictates what color the priest wears during Mass?

37. Are we to only receive communion from a priest?

38. Is a lector allowed to wear a long white robe like a priest?

39. What is the Church teaching about altar girls?

40. What is the difference between a deacon and a brother?

35. Why does the priest wear special ornate clothing during Mass?

I was struggling to answer my five-year-old's question about the priest's outfit at Mass. He wanted to know why Father looked so dressed up. What should I tell him?

Arlene in Layton, Utah

Let's start with a bit of terminology. The special clothing that ministers wear during public prayer is called *vestments*. These are different from both the uniform that a priest would wear in everyday life (black shirt with white collar) and a religious habit worn by a nun, a friar, or a monk. When we say *vestments*, we mean specifically the outer garments worn only during the celebration of certain sacraments or prayer services.

First, why do they seem more fancy, dressy, or ornate? Picture that long white dress that a bride wears on her wedding day. Is that something she would typically show up to work in on a Tuesday? Most likely not. It is designed to look special and to let everyone know that what is happening on this particular day is momentous and life changing. After high school, a good friend of mine entered the Navy. I remember that he had different sets of uniforms. The one he would wear for his day-to-day job was dark and had his name on it. But the nice white uniform, decorated with various colored pins symbolizing his rank and commendations, was reserved for special occasions. When he would put that on, it would signal that something significant was about to happen.

For Catholics, Mass is indeed a special occasion. Vestments are a visual cue that what we are doing in church on Sunday is worthy of our attention, life changing, and not to be confused with the mundane activities of the rest of the week. Mass is also meant to be beautiful, and "the sacred vestments should also contribute to the beauty of the sacred action itself" (*GIRM* 335). I was fortunate enough to see up close some centuries-old, hand-woven silk vestments worn by popes that were on loan for a unique exhibit at the Metropolitan Museum of Art in New York City. My goodness, they were truly breathtaking!

Another thing about vestments is that they vary based on the particular role someone has during Mass. For instance, a priest wears a *stole* (sort of like a decorative scarf that drapes over both shoulders and down the front on each side) with a *chasuble* as the outer layer (similar to a large cape that covers most of his body). Whereas a deacon serving next to him wears something similar (but just slightly different) called a *dalmatic*, designed with large sleeves rather than as a cape, and the deacon's stole drapes on a diagonal across his chest. Altar servers usually wear a simple white robe called an *alb* (from the same root word as *albino*) that appears less ornate than the others I've just mentioned.

It's important to note that the different vestments indicate a different role or function that a particular minister has during the Mass. They are not meant to indicate who is more holy or blessed or closer to God.

36. Is there something that dictates what color the priest wears during Mass?

I am a new Catholic and I just noticed that this Sunday our priest was wearing a different color than he was last week. Is this his personal choice or is there something that regulates what color the priest wears?

Hannah in Knoxville, Tennessee

Welcome to the family, Hannah! I like observant new Catholics. You're right: the priest does sometimes change the color of his vestments, and not merely for the sake of variety or because he's some churchy fashionista. The underlying principle here is that Catholics follow a rhythm throughout the year made up of different seasons interspersed with feast days. This should not be a foreign concept, even to people who don't go to church or believe in God. We look forward to secular holidays and are accustomed to the changing of the earth's seasons and the signs that accompany them. People's wardrobes might include light pastel colors in the spring but darker earth tones in autumn. Back when I was a kid, my mom always told us that we couldn't wear white pants after Labor Day because summer was over. (These days we can most easily tell it's fall when we start seeing ads for pumpkin spice *everything*.)

Our master blueprint for celebrating Mass everywhere in the world, the *General Instruction of the Roman Missal*, teaches, "The purpose of a variety in the color of the sacred vestments is to give effective expression even outwardly to the specific character of the mysteries of faith being celebrated and to a sense of Christian life's passage through the course of the liturgical year" (*GIRM* 345). In other words, the faithful should notice we're in a different Church season when they see a new color.

Okay, so which colors go with what seasons? In Advent and Lent, the priest wears purple (technically violet). Purple has long been a color associated with royalty in many cultures, but since the soldiers mocked Jesus before his crucifixion by dressing him in purple (Mark 15:17–18), it has taken on a meaning of suffering, penance, and anticipation for Christians. Big joyous celebrations like Easter, Christmas, and saint feast days call for white, just like a wedding dress or a formal Navy uniform. Red is rarely worn throughout the year. There is no full season that is assigned to red, only individual feast days. But there is a trick to figuring out which days call for red vestments: just think blood and fire, both (kinda) red. Red days include Passion Sunday and Good Friday, as well as any day commemorating a martyr (someone who has died for the faith). Notice that a common theme here revolves around bloodshed—and blood is red. Fire is a common symbol for the Holy Spirit, so red should also be worn on Pentecost Sunday and Masses that celebrate the sacrament of confirmation. The rest of the time, outside of special seasons or feast days, the color for Mass is green.

But don't fret…neither you nor your parish priest need to memorize all this. The place where the priest gets changed into his vestments for Mass is called a sacristy. In pretty much every sacristy in the world there's a small book—published in the United States by Paulist Press—called the Ordo (or "Order of Prayer"). Along with other pieces of important information, the Ordo tells the celebrant what color to wear each day of the year. Thank God for that! And this is (finally) the answer to your question. This handy little book is what "regulates" the color of the priest's vestments.

37. Are we to only receive communion from a priest?

I read in an article that we should receive communion only from the hands of a priest or deacon. Is that true? What about eucharistic ministers who are laypeople?

Gwen in Mission Viejo, California

Let's start with a couple of definitions, Gwen. You mentioned "eucharistic ministers." That's a term that was popular for many years, but lately we prefer to use the more accurate (if somewhat clunky) designation *extraordinary ministers of Holy Communion*. More wordy, true, but it does actually help in answering your question. In the Church's mind, the *ordinary* minister of Holy Communion—that is, the person who should under normal circumstances be the one distributing communion to the faithful—is the priest who is the main celebrant of the Mass and who just moments earlier consecrated it. Aside from theology, that just makes sense, right? At home, if your grandmother cooked a big festive meal, she would also likely be the one serving it on the family table. Yet you can also imagine a situation where Grandma might enlist some help with the serving, for instance, if she was such a good cook that she opened her own restaurant. Then Nonna would probably hire waiters and waitresses. These are equivalent, in a way, to extraordinary ministers of Holy Communion.

Okay, now to this article you read. If it was an opinion piece where the author was making a case that the Church should change its policy and restrict communion distribution only to ordained ministers, that's one thing. People have a right to their opinions. But I hope it was not an article claiming that it is wrong for you to receive from the hands of a layperson. Because that would be tantamount to saying that the Church's official teaching on this is wrong.

The *Code of Canon Law* of the Catholic Church defines the ordinary minister of Holy Communion as a bishop, priest, or deacon, and "the extraordinary minister of Holy Communion is an acolyte or other member of the Christian faithful" (canon 910). The law specifies, "When the necessity of the church warrants it…lay persons, even if they are not lectors or acolytes can also…distribute Holy Communion" (canon 230, section 3). Lest you think that your pastor can just grab somebody out of the back pew to help with communion on a busy Sunday (even though this is *actually permitted* by *GIRM* 162), the U.S. Bishops' 2001 document called *Norms for the Distribution and Reception of Holy Communion under Both Kinds in the Dioceses of the U.S.A.* insists that "extraordinary ministers of Holy Communion should receive sufficient spiritual, theological, and practical preparation to fulfill their role with knowledge and reverence." In practice, most lay ministers who serve at Mass are very well-trained, take their job seriously, and execute it with reverence and grace.

I think it's clear that the Church would not have all these laws, instructions, and commentaries about laypeople distributing communion if it were true that the congregation is only permitted to receive the Eucharist from the hands of a clergy member. One other guy who's cool with having other people help distribute communion? Jesus. When the Lord performs the miracle of the multiplication of the loaves—a scene in which Catholics see a great many eucharistic undertones—how does he make sure all five thousand people get their share? "Looking up to heaven, he said the blessing, broke the loaves, and gave them to [his] disciples to set before the people" (Mark 6:41). I doubt anyone in that large crowd complained that they got their piece of miraculous bread from some unknown disciple instead of directly from Jesus.

All that having been said, Gwen, when you receive communion at Mass, if you would prefer it be from the priest, that's certainly your choice and there's nothing wrong with that. On occasion when I'm giving out communion, I notice someone doing the old "line switch." You know what I'm talking about? Somebody comes from a different part of the church to intentionally get into my communion line rather than receive from whichever lay minister was assigned to their section. When I see this, I don't make any judgment on that line-switcher. If it's important to them to do that, God bless them. So you, or the author of that article you read, might think, "Hey, that's my priest up there; I love my priest and I love it when he gives me communion." That's wonderful.

However, personal preference is not the same as Church teaching. It is not true that Catholics are only supposed to receive communion from the hands of an ordained person. What matters is that the hands that *consecrated* the Eucharist are those that were anointed with chrism oil at an ordination Mass. And what matters even more than that is Christ's True Presence in the Eucharist. How about we focus on the gift itself rather than the bearer of the gift?

38. Is a lector allowed to wear a long white robe like a priest?

Recently, I went to Mass at a different parish and was surprised to see the female lector was wearing a long white robe like a priest! What's up with *that*?

Joseph in Washington, D.C.

Not what you were expecting, eh? True, what you saw is fairly unusual. But it is allowed and some parishes do have this custom. The changes ushered in by the Second Vatican Council in the 1960s have since empowered devout, talented laypeople to share their many gifts with the community of God's people. And we have become quite accustomed to seeing laypeople up in the sanctuary. But wearing special vestments for Mass is just for the priest and servers, right? Nope.

In fact, the Church permits anyone serving during Mass in any capacity to wear the long white robe called an *alb*. "In the dioceses of the United States of America, acolytes, altar servers, lectors, and other lay ministers may wear the *alb* or other suitable vesture or other appropriate and dignified clothing" (*GIRM* 339).

In my experience, the vast majority of American parishes opt to have only acolytes and altar servers wearing albs, with the rest of the liturgical ministers don-ning what we used to refer to as our "Sunday best" clothing. Some expand this further by asking extraordinary ministers of Holy Communion to wear albs as they perform their ministry at Mass. The rarest—but I have seen it—is what you noticed: the lector also wearing an alb. As you can see above, the *General Instruction* does specifically list lectors as those who may wear an alb.

mass class notes

Liturgical Minister: anyone serving a specific role at Mass like a lector, usher, or music leader

This is because the alb, as a white garment reminiscent of the one we were all given at our baptism, symbolizes our baptismal call to serve. It is for this reason that even priests, deacons, and bishops who vest for Mass will first put on an alb underneath the other decorative layers that go on top. Theologically, this reminds us that the vocation to ordained ministry builds upon the initial call to serve promised at baptism. Because laypeople share with the clergy this baptismal call to ministry through what's known as the "priesthood of all believers," they may properly wear an alb whenever serving at Mass.

On a personal note, my very first Catholic ministry role was as a lector at my confirmation Mass at age thirteen. I wasn't wearing an alb but I was wearing the red robe my whole confirmation class wore that day. I'm pretty sure the Lord was, unbeknownst to me, planting the seeds of a priestly vocation even back then. In a humbling turn of events, I inadvertently switched off the microphone just as I began reading. No one past the first row could hear a thing, including my parents. These days, I speak into a mic that goes up to a satellite allowing my voice to be heard all around the country. God's got quite the sense of humor!

39. What is the Church teaching about altar girls?

We've just moved to a new diocese and for the first time I've seen altar girls serving up there with the priest at Mass. To what degree is this allowed?

Daphne in Boiling Springs, Pennsylvania

First of all, permit me to modify your terminology slightly. While we always used to just say "altar boys," these days we tend to use the more inclusive "altar servers" since the people we're talking about might be either male or female, and they could also be either young people between the ages of eight and fourteen, or adults, even senior citizens, who have been trained to serve at the altar during Mass. But let's rewind a bit.

Prior to fifty years ago, the only people allowed to serve around the altar alongside priests and deacons were young men formally instituted as *acolytes*, who were often those preparing for, or at least potentially discerning, the priesthood. They were dressed kinda like priests, up there assisting the priests, and many of them eventually went on to become priests. A few things have happened over time that have led to you seeing a female altar server at your new parish—none of which are harbingers of women being admitted to the ordained priesthood.

In the early 1970s, the position of acolyte was redefined so that it was no longer one of the "minor orders" on the way to priestly ordination, but rather a role that could be held by anyone trained to carry it out—yet one that was still limited to men. The 1983 revised version of the *Code of Canon Law* eliminated that male-only restriction by allowing anyone to serve in the capacity of acolyte without being officially "installed" as one, including women. Despite a fair amount of ambiguity, this paved the way for many individual American parishes to begin experimenting with what were first known as "altar girls." A decade later, a Vatican proclamation approved by Pope St. John Paul II formally allowed female altar servers throughout the world on a temporary or exceptional basis, leaving the final decision in any diocese up to the bishop. Most recently in 2021, Pope Francis called for a change in the wording of canon law to afford altar servers of either gender equal status in the eyes of the Church on a permanent basis (see canon 230). The Holy Father declared at the time, "Such lay ministries, being based on the sacrament of baptism, can be entrusted to all the faithful who are suitable, whether male or female."

However, it is still up to a local bishop to decide who may perform the role of altar server in his diocese. The generally accepted practice in the United States and around the world, including at papal Masses since the time of Benedict XVI, is to allow women altar servers. Of the more than two hundred dioceses in the United States and Canada, only one or two do not allow female altar servers. In Pope Francis's view, having women serve at the altar has value far beyond the sanctuary of their home parish. He argued that doing so would "increase the recognition…of the precious contribution that many lay people make, including women, to the life and mission of the Church."

40. What is the difference between a deacon and a brother?

I'd like to know the difference between a deacon and a brother in the Catholic Church, and what does the pathway to each look like?

Ben in Tempe, Arizona

A deacon is an ordained minister of the Catholic Church and a brother is not. That doesn't make the role of a brother any less important or desirable, just different.

Let's first talk about deacons. There are two different kinds: transitional deacons and permanent deacons. Transitional deacons are those who are finishing up their seminary training and will soon be ordained to the priesthood. Every priest serves as a deacon first, typically for about six months to a year before their priestly ordination. The deacon's role is truly one of service. In fact, the word *deacon* comes from an ancient Greek word meaning "servant, waiter, or minister." Those who will eventually hold leadership roles in the Church as priests or bishops must begin by taking on the humble role of a servant, and thus imitate Christ (see Philippians 2:5–11).

I remember quite fondly my time as a transitional deacon. I really did love it!

The other type of deacon is a permanent deacon, a married or single, older man with a call to the ordained ministry, but who will not continue on to priesthood. These account for about 30 percent of deacons in the United States. Since the earliest days of Christianity, deacons have served those most in need by visiting the sick and imprisoned. Today, deacons are empowered by the Church to preach, perform baptisms, and witness marriages, and may officiate at a funeral service or burial. Very often you find them assisting the priest at Mass as kind of a "right-hand man."

Brothers do not usually act in any of these capacities. A religious brother or sister is someone who does not receive the sacrament of holy orders, but nonetheless makes a commitment—usually for a lifetime—of living in community and serving the Church. While permanent deacons may be married, a religious brother chooses to live as a celibate. Further, a brother would not necessarily aspire to ordination. I have heard religious brothers describe it this way: "A priest answers the vocation to be a father, a leader. I feel more called to walk alongside the laypeople—more like a sibling than a parent." Hence the terms *brother* versus *father*.

A fair analogy might be the distinction found in the military between officers and enlisted. These are separate tracks in which one can choose to serve. It would not be fair to say that someone who achieves the rank of master sergeant in the Marines couldn't cut it as a first lieutenant, even though technically the latter outranks the former in the military hierarchy. Most prefer to look at it as a different call to serve with different gifts in a different way.

Some men's religious orders have both brothers and priests, the Benedictine monks for example. Others are entire communities of just brothers, such as the Christian Brothers. And there are also men's communities like my own, the Paulist Fathers, who do not offer a brother track. The particular work of a religious brother will vary. In a monastic setting (like the Benedictines), brothers might take up activities that sustain the abbey like farming, bread or jam making, brewing beer, or they may serve their fellow monks by cooking, cleaning, or carpentry. A member of the Christian Brothers would very likely end up teaching or administering in one of the Catholic schools they run. I know brothers who work in vocation ministry (recruiting), in parish-based adult education, and some who are full-time icon artists and church music composers.

The journey toward becoming a brother or a deacon varies a bit. In general, to become ordained as a permanent deacon, you would go through your Catholic diocese. There will likely be several years of preparation and study at the master's degree level. In many dioceses, a deacon's wife would be part of the formation program and the discernment process—she may even attend classes with her husband. If you contact the diocese where you live, you can find out about the procedure, requirements, how long it takes, and so on.

The path to becoming a religious brother includes joining a particular religious community of other men. It may or may not involve as much academic study, but it will require you to profess celibacy. So these are very different paths. If you think you might have a call to live life as a religious brother (or sister), I like to recommend VocationMatch.com, a great online resource created by the folks at the National Religious Vocation Conference. It's well suited to people who don't even really know what religious life is all about, let alone the distinctions between all the different communities one can join.

So, Ben, if you've asked this question because you are feeling the Holy Spirit nudging you to pursue a religious vocation, let me encourage you to keep listening to that call and keep taking steps forward! The Church needs you and your gifts!

PART 6

The Word

41. Why are there so many Scripture readings at Mass?

42. Why can't the priest pick his own Scripture readings?

43. How much of the Bible is used for the readings at Mass?

44. Why do we call it the "responsorial psalm"?

45. Why do we hear so much from St. Paul during Mass and not from other saints?

46. Why do we make a big deal about reading the Gospel?

47. What are those mini Signs of the Cross we make right before the Gospel is read?

48. What is the difference between a homily and a sermon?

49. What guidelines does the Church give for homilies?

50. Why doesn't the Creed include anything about the Eucharist?

41. Why are there so many Scripture readings at Mass?

Can you tell me why we have three separate readings from Scripture at Mass? This seems like a lot. Shouldn't we be more focused on the Eucharist?

Janine, driving through southern Illinois

I'll start with a couple of modifications to your math, Janine. Depending on how we count, we could actually say that we have *four* distinct proclamations of the Scriptures at Sunday Mass. That figure would include the responsorial psalm, which comes between the first and second readings, because the psalms are found in the Bible. To be fair, that is something of a nuance since even the Church herself doesn't refer to the proclamation of the psalm as a "reading," but treats it more like a prayer of the congregation. The terms we use are *the first reading, the responsorial psalm, the second reading,* and *the Gospel reading.* All of those are heard on a Sunday or big feast day. At daily Mass during the week, there is one less reading.

Okay, enough of the Mass math. Why do we hear multiple selections from the Bible during the same Mass? First and foremost, despite a stereotypical reputation to the contrary, this is because the Scriptures are very important to the faith life of Catholics. Our *Catechism* teaches, "In Sacred Scripture, the Church constantly finds her nourishment and her strength, for she welcomes it not as a human word, but as what it really is, the Word of God. In the sacred books, the Father who is in heaven comes lovingly to meet his children, and talks with them" (*CCC* 104). Wow, just picture that for a moment: the God who created the universe and has existed since before time began comes down from the heavens to little ol' you and me and strikes up a conversation! Like a loving parent, God shares with us the story of our family history, he gives us sage advice on how to live, challenges us to do better, and promises to always be there for us. When? How? Through the Scriptures. When we crack open our Bibles at home, when we hear the readings at Mass, we believe it's like God speaking directly to each of us, to all of us. Seems like that's something it would behoove us to make time for. So, the Church wisely offers us generous helpings of God's word at Mass.

Indeed, the most fundamental way to break down the parts of the Mass would be to divide it in two: (1) the first half is devoted to our taking in the Word of God through the readings and the homily (which is why we call the first half of Mass the Liturgy of the Word); and (2) the second half is when we receive our Lord's True Presence in communion (the Liturgy of the Eucharist). While these two may not time out to precisely the same length, the Church places equal importance on them both. Furthermore, we see the two halves, Word and Sacrament, as inextricably linked: "The Church has always

> **mass class notes**
>
> **Homily:**
> preaching on the day's readings by the priest or deacon (for more, see question 48 below)

116

venerated the Scriptures as she venerates the Lord's Body. She never ceases to present to the faithful the bread of life, taken from the one table of God's Word and Christ's Body" (*CCC* 103).

Even the Lord's presence at Mass is not limited to the consecrated bread and wine. "In the readings, as explained by the homily, God speaks to his people, opening up to them the mystery of redemption and salvation, and offering them spiritual nourishment; and *Christ himself is present in the midst of the faithful through his word*" (*GIRM* 55, emphasis added). In some of the Mass prayers, the priest says, "Blessed indeed is your Son, present in our midst when we are gathered by his love, and when, as once for the disciples, so now for us, he opens the Scriptures and breaks the bread" (*Roman Missal*, "Eucharistic Prayers for Various Needs and Occasions, I-IV"). This last line is an allusion to the very powerful gospel story referred to as the Road to Emmaus (Luke 24:13–35). In it, we hear about the resurrected Jesus walking alongside two disciples while opening their minds to the Scriptures before sitting down with them at table to break the bread. It is then that they recognize he is there with them and immediately recall how their hearts were burning inside as he had earlier proclaimed and explained Scripture to them. For Catholics, this is a eucharistic passage in the Bible that underscores the intimate and necessary connection between what happens at the ambo (lectern) and what happens at the altar. We spend time with God's Word so that we can more deeply appreciate the gift we receive in the Eucharist and know how to live Christian lives after having taken Christ into our very selves.

Because of the great value the Church places on the Word of God, the bishops and other leaders who gathered for the Second Vatican Council in the mid-1960s decided to add more Scripture readings to the Mass and draw from a larger portion of the Bible. The first reading is almost always taken from the Old Testament (the exception being the seven weeks following Easter Sunday when we hear from the Acts of the Apostles, stories of the early

Church). The second reading comes from the New Testament (but not the Gospels), usually a selection from one of St. Paul's letters to the Christian communities he founded. Finally, there is a proclamation from one of the four Gospels: Matthew, Mark, Luke, or John. Just as important as the Bible passages themselves is the homily that follows, which (ideally) enables the ancient words of the Scriptures to be understood and applied by modern congregations, inspiring, affirming, and challenging Catholics to live lives that flow from their faith.

On a personal note, the Scriptures have always been very important to me. My role as a lector at Mass, particularly in my college and young adult years, as well as my participation in Bible study groups with both Catholic and non-Catholic friends, were essential precursors to my answering the call to the priesthood.

42. Why can't the priest pick his own Scripture readings?

Sometimes we go to my girlfriend's Christian church where the preacher decides which passages from the Bible he will preach on each week. I'm pretty sure Catholic priests are not allowed to choose their own readings, right? Why not?

Mark in College Station, Texas

Aha! Your question is a perfect illustration of why we Catholics use a lectionary, a book with an ordered sequence of biblical readings with particular days assigned to each. You're correct: a Catholic priest or deacon may not just flip through the Bible and select a passage to preach on. They must use the assigned readings for that Sunday or weekday found in the lectionary. *Oh boy, once again the Catholic Church is limiting our freedom with its rules!* Well, not really. I find several very compelling reasons for following the readings set forth in the lectionary.

First of all, let's start with the very word *catholic*. It means "universal." Among other benefits of a universal Church is that you have the assurance that the people in the parish on the other side of town—as well as Catholics on the other side of the world—are hearing the very same readings you are on any given Sunday (weekday Masses, too). What good is that? Even if you don't call up your second cousin in Poland and say, "Hey, what did you think of that passage from Ezekiel at Mass this morning?" you are still bonded with them through a common experience. You probably have seen the ubiquitous aphorism "always remember we are under the same sky looking at the same moon" on greeting cards or coffee mugs or in movies. Human beings long to be connected. If we can feel a common bond with someone far away merely by glancing toward the sky at night, how much more connected could we feel by simultaneously listening to the same inspiring and challenging words from God?

As a matter of fact, looking to a lectionary for the Sunday Scripture readings doesn't just create community among us Catholics. Many other Christian denominations follow the *Revised Common Lectionary*, which, with a few exceptions, contains the same Bible passages in the same order on the same Sundays as our *Catholic Lectionary for Mass*. These churches include United Methodist, Presbyterian, Disciples of Christ, American Baptist, Reformed Church in America, Episcopal, Lutheran, United Church of Christ, and more. There are two billion Christians on the planet. Imagine the power of even half of them being moved by and acting on a common passage of Scripture heard on the same day!

Another reason is that there is intent behind which readings have been chosen for which days. "The arrangement of biblical readings provides the faithful with a knowledge of the whole of God's Word, in a pattern suited to the purpose. Throughout the liturgical year, but above all during the seasons of Easter, Lent, and Advent, the choice and sequence of readings are aimed at giving Christ's faithful an ever-deepening perception of the faith they profess and of the history of salvation" (*General Introduction to the Lectionary for Mass*, 60). In other words, we've given this some thought—for centuries, actually. It's kind of like a seasoned college professor putting together a well-ordered syllabus for the semester: it's been designed, tried, and tested so the students can have the maximum benefit of learning.

Now, Mark, we get back to why I said your question is right on. Using a lectionary makes sure that a greater portion of God's Word is heard by the faithful. Really? Yes. Over the course of the three-year lectionary cycle for Sundays, Catholics oftentimes hear more of and a greater variety of the Scriptures than those who attend so-called Bible churches. Why? Because having the passages assigned helps us avoid the temptation to just hear what we want to hear from God. It's often said that good preaching should "comfort the afflicted and afflict the comfortable," but very few people go to church to be made uncomfortable. And I can tell you from experience, neither do we preachers enjoy making you squirm. It's not easy for any priest or minister to get up in front of a wealthy congregation and preach on a biblical passage where God really seems to favor the poor over the rich. It's really hard to hear "love your enemies" from the pulpit the day after a terrorist attack. Given the choice, it is my firm belief that the majority of preachers and congregations would choose to steer clear from the parts of the Bible that push us out of our comfort zones.

A few years ago I took a good friend to see Billy Joel in concert at Madison Square Garden in New York City. It was a fun evening! Before starting the show, the Piano Man polled the audience. "I have two set lists prepared for tonight. One has a bunch of my most popular songs mixed in with some deep cuts and rarities. The other set list is just one big hit after another." The audience voted overwhelmingly, by applause and cheering, that we just wanted him to "play the hits." That is our tendency with God's Word, I'm afraid. A lectionary forces us to explore those "deep cuts" in the Scriptures that may not immediately give us a warm and fuzzy affirmation. Both the preacher and the gathered assembly are often made to stretch a little bit when none of us has the choice of what readings we will need to wrestle with that day. And it's in the stretching that we grow. A lectionary empowers us to grow as believers because it doesn't let us simply "play the hits."

43. How much of the Bible is used for the readings at Mass?

I have heard that we Catholics read more of the Bible than some "Bible-believing" Protestant churches do. How much of the Bible do we hear from if we go to Mass every Sunday? Do we read through the whole Bible in a year?

Sophia in Fair Haven, New Jersey

Because there are so many different Christian denominations, nondenominational, and congregational churches, all with varying practices, there's no way to compare what the Catholic Church does to all of them. Do we get exposed to more of the Bible at our Masses than *some* of them? I'm sure that's true. What we can be more precise about is comparing our own current Liturgy of the Word to what it was like sixty or more years ago. On that front, I've got good news and bad news.

The bad news (you notice how people always start with the bad news?) is that you will definitely not hear the entire Bible read over the course of one year, even if you're going to Mass every day. If you really would like to do that, there are some great page-a-day devotionals and podcasts out there that can take you on a yearlong journey through all the books of Scripture. Further, I've read on some websites the erroneous claim that we Catholics will get to hear the entire Bible in three years if we go to Mass every day. Sorry, but that is what has become known as "fake news." Truth is, it's not even close.

The good news is that we do hear much more of the Bible proclaimed at Mass than we used to. The Mass as we celebrated it from the sixteenth century up until about

mass class notes

Liturgy of the Word: roughly the first half of Mass, largely consisting of the readings and the homily

sixty years ago had fewer readings, and the passages themselves were drawn from a narrower section of the Scriptures and were repeated more frequently. The Second Vatican Council (1962–65) made it a priority to give Catholics a much greater exposure to the Word of God when they come to church. "The treasures of the Bible are to be opened up more lavishly so that a richer fare may be provided for the faithful at the table of God's Word. In this way the more significant parts of sacred Scripture will be read to the people over a fixed number of years" (Constitution on the Sacred Liturgy, *Sacrosanctum Concilium* 51).

Our current *Catholic Lectionary for Mass*, first brought into use in 1969, opened up the biblical treasures in many ways. We now use a three-year cycle for readings on Sundays and a two-year cycle for daily Mass readings. Previously, the same readings were repeated every year and weekdays and Sundays were treated the same. Whereas we used to only hear one reading before the Gospel on Sundays, we now are treated to two separate readings, one from the Old Testament and one from parts of the New Testament other than the Gospels. These two used to share one spot, and very little of the Old Testament made the cut. Even when it came to the Gospels, there was a paucity being proclaimed in the old Mass. For example, prior to 1969, someone going to church all the time would only hear about 3 percent of the Gospel of Mark. Nowadays, if you attend Mass every day, you'll eventually take in over 96 percent of Mark's words. All told, the reforms of Vatican II added to the Mass over 3,000 verses of Scripture from the Old Testament and more than 4,300 from the New Testament (a verse is about a sentence or two).

None of that, however, addresses the question of *how much* of the Bible we get to hear at Mass. To answer this with any kind of accuracy, I turned to a priest who has a far greater tolerance for math than I do (this book is called *Mass Class* not *Math Class*!). Jesuit priest and statistician Father Felix Just, SJ, PhD, has crunched the numbers and produced all kinds of tables filled with lectionary stats on the website catholic-resources.org. According to his research, a Catholic who attends Mass every Sunday and holy day of obligation (something we're all supposed to do, by the way) during the three-year reading cycle will hear about 41 percent of the New Testament but a mere 3.7 percent of the Old Testament, not including the Psalms, which are prayed at every Mass. Devout Mass goers who show up on weekdays, even though they don't have to, are awarded a scriptural bonus: they get to hear 71.5 percent of the New Testament and 13.5 percent of the Old (again, apart from the Psalms). That may sound pretty low, but for context, prior to 1969 it was 16.5 percent of the New Testament and, get this, less than 1 percent of the Old Testament.

Bottom line: less than one-third of the Bible is ever proclaimed at Mass. You won't hear more than that if you stick around longer, even for decades. But we hope you do!

44. Why do we call it the "responsorial psalm"?

Recently, I attended Sunday Mass at a church that's not my home parish. They did something I've never seen before and I'm wondering if it's okay. After the first reading, the small choir (they called it a scola) chanted the verses to the psalm, but they never invited the congregation to join in. I thought it was called the "responsorial psalm" because we get to respond. But we didn't! Is this an approved way of praying the psalm?

Kurt in Burlington, Vermont

This is an interesting question. Let's start with, why is it called the "responsorial psalm"? I bet a lot of Catholics would get that answer wrong on a Mass Class quiz (and now maybe you're wondering if there will be one at the end of this book!). What likely leads us astray is the fact that very often in Catholic parishes the responsorial psalm is prayed in a sort of call-and-response format. By that I mean, whether it is spoken or sung, usually the leader invites the congregation to "repeat after me." This works well for the Psalms because they were originally written as poetry and most often chanted or sung when prayed, even thousands of years ago. These days, typically the cantor or choir will be responsible for singing or chanting the verses of the selected psalm and encouraging the entire assembly to join in for the antiphon (the one line that will be repeated, kind of like the refrain or "chorus" in a pop song). I'm assuming this is the kind of thing you were expecting when you went to that other Catholic parish.

Given that this back-and-forth between the leader and the congregation is our most common experience of the responsorial psalm—even when it is spoken, not sung—it's natural for us to conclude that the name *responsorial* is meant to describe the people responding to the leader with "their part," the antiphon. But actually, that's not it.

It's called the responsorial psalm because it is a *response* to the Scripture reading that has just come before it (in most cases, a passage from the Old Testament). It is the gathered assembly responding to the Word of God: an opportunity to both meditate on the biblical passage (see *GIRM* 61) and for us, the entire congregation, to affirm, ratify, and take ownership of the message just proclaimed in our midst. This is a familiar rhythm repeated throughout the Mass: a *proclamation* by a single person or a select few, followed by an *acclamation* by all the people. The most obvious version of this pattern is when the priest alone prays a prayer and then the people respond with "Amen."

Think of attending a Broadway show or a high school play. At the end, when the performers have finished speaking all their lines, the audience, who has largely been quiet up to this point, erupts in applause or shouts "Bravo!" This is the moment when the people in the seats get to respond by showing their appreciation, or by indicating that they resonate with what they have just experienced or that what was spoken has moved them in some way. All of our "amens" and other acclamations during Mass are ways that we, God's people, respond to what is being read, preached, said, or prayed and take ownership of it for ourselves (see *GIRM* 35–37).

THE WORD

Okay, back to the responsorial psalm, and to your initial question about it being acceptable for the cantor or music group to sing or chant the psalm alone without any participation from the assembly. Here's a pretty clear answer from the primary source:

> There are two established ways of singing the psalm after the first reading: responsorially and directly. In responsorial singing, which, as far as possible, is to be given preference, the psalmist, or cantor of the psalm, sings the psalm verse and the whole congregation joins in by singing the response. In direct singing of the psalm there is no intervening response by the community; either the psalmist, or cantor of the psalm, sings the psalm alone as the community listens or else all sing it together. (*Lectionary for Mass*, Introduction, 20)

The call-and-response method most of us are used to has indeed been "given preference" as directed by the lectionary. In my estimation it is by far the more common of the two ways. It is also a clearer expression of an acclamation by all the people in response to something proclaimed by one person, the reading of the Old Testament passage by the lector. However, as you can see, the Church does allow the alternative version of praying the psalm that you experienced recently. In fact, the *General Instruction* treats the two options as fairly evenly weighted: "The entire congregation…takes part by singing the response, except when the Psalm is sung straight through without a response" (*GIRM* 61). The latter approach emphasizes a meditative response to the first reading on the part of the community rather than a vocal one. Granted, it's not as vociferous as shouting "Bravo!" but it has the possibility of being even more profound.

45. Why do we hear so much from St. Paul during Mass and not from other saints?

I love St. Francis, but I never hear any readings from him during Mass. Yet I hear from St. Paul almost every week. Why is the liturgy so focused on Paul? Couldn't we take the readings from a variety of saints?

Adrienne in Victoria, British Columbia, Canada

I'm gonna try not to be biased because I am a Paulist priest and I love St. Paul. Luckily, the reply to your question will not have to do with any preference of mine—or yours for that matter. The answer is simple: St. Francis didn't write the Bible! At Mass, the readings are taken from the Scriptures. It so happens that the authors of some parts of the Bible are also saints. So, I can see why it might lead one to think that we are hearing from this saint or that saint. But it's really not about the human authors at all. For thousands of years, when people of faith have gathered for public prayer and worship, they have wanted to hear what God has to say to them (see Exodus 24:7.) Catholics believe that God is present to us at Mass in the proclamation of his Word (see *GIRM* 55). Yes, the preaching and the writings of all the saints have value and can draw us closer to God. But the Church does not teach that the words of the saints are equivalent to the Sacred Scriptures, which we believe are "authored by God" (see *CCC* 105).

"Okay," you're wondering, "but we do have several readings at each Mass; couldn't we on occasion just substitute one of them with something else of spiritual value?" Well...nope. The *General Instruction* warns that it is "unlawful to substitute other texts" (*GIRM* 57) in place of the Scripture readings. The *Lectionary* itself goes even further: "In the celebration of Mass the biblical readings...may not be omitted, shortened, or, worse still, replaced by nonbiblical readings" (*Lectionary for Mass*, Introduction, 12). "Worse still"?! Yikes. Sounds like the Church is pretty firm on this point.

But wait a minute: if you're listening to your favorite 80s music radio station (one of my presets, for sure!) and they discreetly slip in "Sunday Morning" by Maroon 5 between classics by Madonna and Depeche Mode, you would be justified in complaining to the program director that a song from 2002 does not belong! There are plenty of other places you can hear hits by Maroon 5, just not on an 80s station. Lest you accuse me of trivializing the Mass by that analogy, my point is that if we accept "no substitutions" when it comes to musical entertainment, it shouldn't seem unreasonable to preclude swapping out the Bible readings at Mass.

What about your complaint, er, "observation," that there is a preponderance of Paul read at Mass?

mass class notes

Lectionary:
book that contains all the Scripture readings and Psalm responses divided up into passages for each Mass

You're right about that! Part of the reason for this is mathematical. Of the twenty-seven books of the New Testament, thirteen are either written by or attributed to St. Paul: by word count that's just over 24 percent. But the major contributing factor was a decision made by those who created the lectionary in the 1960s. They decided then that the second reading at Sunday Mass would be taken from the New Testament, but not from the Gospels (which have their own separate slot) or Acts of the Apostles or Revelation—essentially limiting the selection to the "epistles" or letters, the vast majority of which are Paul's.

Having said all that, there are still opportunities to hear from other saints at Mass, like your fave, St. Francis. The most obvious time is during the homily. The preacher might very well quote from saints and various other sources as he's expounding on the Scriptures. Beyond that, some of the words of saints have been set to music and appear in the hymns we sing at Mass. In fact, our music ministers would likely point out that it's far easier for us to retain song lyrics than mere words read aloud to us. How many Catholics could recount verbatim the words to "Make Me a Channel of Your Peace" (aka the "Prayer of St. Francis")? I think the answer is, way more than could quote a passage from St. Paul off the top of their head.

I'll add one more thing, Adrienne, precisely because you used the word *liturgy* in your question. As you probably know, that's Catholic jargon meaning the public prayer of the Church. Many people use it as a synonym for *Mass*, but in fact it is a much broader term. Case in point, one of the other ways Christians have been praying together for centuries is the Liturgy of the Hours. Monks, nuns, priests, religious, and laypeople pray the Psalms at different times of the day, often in groups (like in a monastery or in a parish setting). You might know this as Morning Prayer or Evening Prayer or Vespers. Collectively, these (and a few more) opportunities to come together for prayer are known as the Liturgy of the Hours. One of these "hours" is the Office of Readings, which contains excerpts from writings and homilies of a great variety of saints. In fact, Adrienne, if you go to church on the feast day of St. Francis, you might get your pet blessed, but you still will not hear any readings from him at Mass. But you *will* be treated to a passage from one of his public letters if you or your parish pray the Office of Readings that day. And because you've put up with a very long answer from me, here it is:

> Furthermore, let us produce worthy fruits of penance. Let us also love our neighbors as ourselves. Let us have charity and humility. Let us give alms because these cleanse our souls from the stains of sin....We must not be wise and prudent according to the flesh. Rather we must be simple, humble and pure." ("A Letter from St. Francis of Assisi to All the Faithful" found in the Office of Readings, *Liturgy of the Hours*, October 4, Memorial of St. Francis)

46. Why do we make a big deal about reading the Gospel?

It seems like we make a bigger deal about the reading from the Gospel during Mass than the other readings. Why is that?

Sheldon in Palo Alto, California

You have observed well. We do make something of a fuss over the reading of the Gospel, much more so than that of the other Scripture readings. Why? Simply because the four Gospels chronicle the miraculous birth, life, ministry, suffering, death, and resurrection of our Lord. They contain the words and works of Jesus himself, as documented by his contemporaries and disciples. Accordingly, the *General Instruction of the Roman Missal* calls the proclamation of the Gospel the "high point" of the Liturgy of the Word (the first half of Mass) and advises that "great reverence is to be shown to it by setting it off from the other readings" (*GIRM* 60).

And set it off we do—in quite a few ways. The most obvious, and perhaps the most effective in terms of getting us to pay more attention, is that the priest, servers, other ministers, and entire gathered assembly stand up when the Gospel is read (not so for the other readings). In addition, the proclamation of the Gospel at Mass is reserved for a member of the clergy (a deacon is preferred, but in his absence, the priest) who even prays a special prayer of worthiness prior to doing so. There is also a procession accompanied by a musical rendition of the ancient word of praise, "Alleluia!" This can be as simple as the priest walking over from his presider's chair to the ambo during the music; or the procession can be more embellished by the deacon or priest holding high in the air a special book that only contains Gospel passages, even parading it all around the church on special occasions. Next, there's a more elaborate introduction to the reading that involves a dialogue with the people ("The Lord be with you," "And with your spirit"), the likes of which only happens at key moments in the Mass. At the conclusion of the reading, the people's response gets an upgrade from "Thanks be to God" to "Praise to you, Lord Jesus Christ!" Then we get to sit down.

On top of all that, depending on your parish, your church design, or other factors, you may even witness one or more of these other flourishes: altar servers holding lit candles may walk alongside the deacon during the procession and even continue to flank the Gospel book while the reading is proclaimed (a long passage will surely test the physical stamina of even the most seasoned altar server); incense may be waved over the open Gospel page (listen for the "clink, clink, clink" over the sound system); the entire Gospel passage may be chanted or sung by a deacon so qualified; if your bishop is presiding, the deacon will likely bring the Book of the Gospels back over to the chair so that the bishop may venerate (kiss) the page from which God's Word

mass class notes

Book of the Gospels: large ornate book containing only Gospel passages, and used in procession was just proclaimed. Oh, and one more. Some older churches, particularly in Europe, contain an extra architectural element: an even more ornate and usually elevated pulpit that is only used for proclaiming the Gospel and preaching. These quite frequently will have something like a circular staircase leading up to them, and they are often adorned with some images of the four Gospel writers or their symbolic representations. These churches would still have an ambo, a lectern where the other readings are proclaimed, but the "high pulpit" is yet another way the Church elevates the experience of the Gospel proclamation—in this case, literally.

The mother church of my community, St. Paul the Apostle Church in New York City, was designed in the late nineteenth century with the high pulpit in the middle, on the right side about halfway back. In the days before microphones the preacher could use the natural projection of his voice placed in the acoustical "sweet spot" of the space so that the entire congregation—even those in the way back—could hear the Gospel and the homily. The wooden steps creak like a haunted house when we put it to use these days for special liturgies such as the Easter Vigil Mass.

Why all the hullabaloo? Think of the Gospel as the "main attraction" of the first half of Mass (sorry, preachers, not the homily). In fact, the Church teaches us that "the other readings, in their established sequence from the Old to the New Testament, prepare the assembly" for the pinnacle: the reading of the Gospel (see *Lectionary for Mass*, Introduction, 13).

If you're the type to arrive at the movie theater with a little time to spare, you're familiar with all "pre-show entertainment": trailers for other movies, glistening close-ups of ice-cold soda, even local real estate ads. During all these, the lights usually remain on, people are still crawling over you to make it to their seats, and there's probably a fair amount of conversation happening. But when it's time for the "feature presentation," the reason why you came, the lights go out, the curtains pull back wider, people settle themselves, and you might even hear one or two anonymous cinematic

135

connoisseurs emit a *shhhh!* All that has preceded was somewhat entertaining (sometimes the local real estate ads are better than the previews), and in a way eased you into what is to come. But now it's time for the main event, and all those little changes let the crowd know the best part is now upon us. That's why we sprinkle in a few bells and whistles before the Gospel is read. Most analogies are imperfect, and this one is not meant to diminish what precedes the Gospel by comparing it to footage of popcorn being popped, but I hope it helps.

So yes, we do make much ado about the Gospel reading—much ado about something vital to the celebration of the Mass.

47. What are those mini Signs of the Cross we make right before the Gospel is read?

I have a question about something I do at Mass but don't know why. Just before our deacon reads the Gospel passage, we all make three mini Signs of the Cross on our forehead, mouth, and chest. Why do we do that?

Dana in Charleston, South Carolina

Ah yes. One of the things we do all the time by rote but…why? Always good to ask that. Let's jump right to the primary source. The *Order of Mass* gives this instruction: "After the deacon or priest gives the invocation, 'A reading from the holy Gospel according to…,' he makes the sign of the cross on the book and, together with the people, on his forehead, lips, and breast. At the same time, the people acclaim: 'Glory to you, O Lord.'" Although not specified there, traditional practice has you make these three mini Signs of the Cross with just your thumb.

THE WORD

While there is no particular verbal prayer the Church pro-scribes to accompany this ritual action (other than "Glory to you, O Lord"), I usually encourage people to silently pray this: "May the Word of God come alive in my mind, on my lips, and in my heart." If you think about it, all three are very important. We surely need to *understand* the Scriptures properly—Lord knows, there have been countless people down through the ages who have mis-interpreted and abused the biblical texts. Yet if we merely hear it, think about it, or study it academically, we may not be allowing the Word of God to come alive in us (see Hebrews 4:12). It needs to also penetrate our *heart*. It needs to change who we are. We should fall more in love with Jesus when we hear the Gospel proclaimed.

But let's circle back to the one in the middle, the one that as Catholics we're probably most reticent to embrace: *on my lips*. We are called to share the good news, to spread the Word. Jesus gave some challenging marching orders to his initial followers that still apply to all believers even two millennia later: "Go into the whole world and proclaim the gospel to every creature" (Mark 16:15; see also Matthew 28:19). Notice the verb *proclaim*. Not *wish* that other people come to God, or merely *pray* for them. We cannot fulfill Christ's Great Commission by keeping our faith to ourselves. St. Paul tries to stir the flame by claiming, "We are ambassadors for Christ, as if God were appealing through us" (2 Corinthians 5:20).

As the Gospel passage is about to be read at Mass, we remind ourselves with these mini Signs of the Cross over three parts of our body that God's Word is not intended to remain lying dormant on the printed page, nor even inside my head or heart. It also must come alive in all areas of my life. "Be doers of the word and not hearers only, deluding yourselves" (James 1:22).

Does that mean that every Catholic Christian needs to stand on a street corner with a megaphone quoting Bible verses or *Cate-chism* chapters? No. But consider this: if the only time you ever say the name "Jesus Christ" aloud is when you stub your toe, maybe it's time that your faith comes alive on your lips.

I really try to be deliberate when I make those mini Signs of the Cross, allowing the profundity of the simple action to sink in and reflecting on ways I could do a better job of letting the Word come alive in my mind, on my lips, and in my heart.

48. What is the difference between a homily and a sermon?

I'm not Catholic, but I love to listen to your show. I have a question. I hear you often talk about your homilies, but when my pastor preaches on Sunday, we call that a sermon. Is there a difference, or is homily *just a Catholic term for the same thing?*

Kathryn in Tuscaloosa, Alabama

First of all, Kathryn, thank you for listening and for your interest in our Catholic experience and traditions. And I'm glad you're asking this question because it's probably one of those things we Catholics wouldn't think to explain. The words *homily* and *sermon* are sometimes used synonymously (even occasionally by priests!), and they do both refer to preaching that happens in the context of public prayer. But technically they are different.

The simplest way to distinguish them is this: a *sermon* is preached on a topic using Scripture passages selected to support its thesis, whereas a *homily* is preached on predetermined readings that the preacher does not choose. When preparing a homily, it is the Catholic preacher's job—with the help of the Holy Spirit, of course!—to draw a theme or cohesive message from the assigned readings of the day. A Christian pastor writing a sermon would typically begin with the basic message they want to convey (or that which God has put on their heart) and then scour his or her Bible for a few passages that can be woven together to reinforce their theme, also with the inspiration of the Spirit. To be fair, I am oversimplifying the oftentimes multifaceted preparation process of both to more clearly illustrate the difference between the two.

A few caveats. It would be inaccurate to say that every time a Catholic preaches that it's necessarily a homily. There are some occasions when a priest or deacon might not preach on the assigned readings but rather offer some appropriate teaching or instruction from the pulpit. Vice versa, there are many Christian denominational churches that do follow a lectionary and therefore those congregations would be hearing homilies. There are advantages to each as well. A sermon series, where the preacher will address a topic or a group of related topics over the course of several Sundays, can be an effective tool for teaching and spiritual renewal with the side benefit of bringing people back to church week after week. On the other hand, a homily that stays true to preaching on the readings of the day, and also addresses the current life experience of the congregation, is a strong testament to the fact that it's really the Holy Spirit connecting the Word of God to the people, and not so much we ministers doing that.

Simply put, while the approaches are from different directions, the end goal of either a homily or a sermon is the same: breaking open the Scriptures and showing their relevance to the lives of those listening.

49. What guidelines does the Church give for homilies?

Over the years I've noticed that priests' homilies can vary greatly in length, content, and, let's say, quality. Does preaching entirely depend on the skills and preferences of the preacher, or does the Church give some guidelines?

Rosalie in Lafayette, Louisiana

Much could be said about Catholic preaching. It is something extremely important to me personally, as well as to my religious community, the Paulist Fathers. A good friend of mine wrote his doctoral thesis on the theology of Catholic preaching of just one of our professors from seminary. And it would probably be most beneficial to hear feedback from the People of God about homilies, rather than another priest (me) prattling on about them. So, I'll just try to stick to answering your specific question.

Yes, the Church does offer some guidelines for homilies, but they are intentionally somewhat ambiguous because so many factors can greatly affect preaching. These can include the culture of a region or even an individual parish, the oratory skills of the preacher, the particular topics he is passionate about, the various types of communication or media that the congregation is used to consuming, and many more. The Church knows and makes allowances for this. Molding and forming someone into an effective preacher is something that begins with seminary training, but oftentimes extends well into his life and ministry. Hence, the guidance from the universal Church errs on the side of broad brushstrokes, rather than narrow prescriptions.

The *General Instruction of the Roman Missal* calls the homily "a living commentary on the word of God" (*GIRM* 29) and recommends that "it should be an exposition of some aspect of the readings from Sacred Scripture...and should take into account both the mystery being celebrated and the particular needs of the listeners" (*GIRM* 65). As I said, fairly nonspecific. The *Lectionary* drills down a bit more: "[The homily] must always lead the community of the faithful to celebrate the Eucharist actively, 'so that they may hold fast in their lives to what they have grasped by faith.' From this living explanation, the Word of God proclaimed in the readings and the Church's celebration of the day's Liturgy will have greater impact" (*Lectionary for Mass*, Introduction, 24).

One thing that stands out to me in both of those is the emphasis on the community that is receiving the preaching.

A homily is not a lecture on doctrine, it is not a Bible study, it is not a political stump speech. It should not feel like you're in a classroom with a teacher up front; in a comedy club on a Friday night; sitting through your uncle's tired old stories at Thanksgiving; or listening to someone's podcast featuring their rambling opinions on the world.

mass class notes

Liturgy:
any public prayer of the Church, but sometimes used as a synonym for *Mass*

That is not to say that a good homily should *never* include elements of teaching, humor, storytelling, politics, personal opinion, explaining the Scriptures, or professing Church doctrine. All of those have their place to varying degrees. But *primarily* the task of the preacher is to help the people in the congregation see more clearly God's presence and action in their daily lives in light of the Scripture passages they have just heard.

This, I would say, is the main takeaway of the U.S. Bishops' 1982 pastoral document called *Fulfilled in Your Hearing: The Homily in the Sunday Assembly* (*FIYH*). It served as the main source of our preaching education when I was in seminary and provides valuable direction for all Catholic preachers. In *FIYH*, the bishops focus first on the assembly, then the preacher himself, then the homily. This approach is laudable (if not a bit surprising), partly because it resonates with what I learned my first year as a communications major at Syracuse University: any type of successful communication needs to take into account the three elements of *sender-message-receiver*. When I prepare a homily, I always take some time to reflect on what's going on in the world or in people's lives *right now* that would connect with the Sunday Scriptures. The preacher is described in *Fulfilled in Your Hearing* as a "mediator of meaning." "The preacher acts as a mediator, making connections between the real lives of people who believe in Jesus Christ but are not always sure what difference faith can make in their lives, and the God who calls us into ever deeper communion with himself and with one another" (*FIYH* 8).

I see my job on the pulpit as a sort of interpreter. Even if you've never heard me preach, you'll notice in this book that I tend to use "real world" analogies and examples. These I believe are effective tools at making the connection between churchy concepts about our faith and how everyday humans usually think and speak; between a transcendent, loving, merciful God and little ol' you and me who are flawed, hurting, and wandering through life. Jesus helped the gathered crowds understand his novel proposition of the "kingdom of God" by talking about seeds and mud, farmers and landowners, fathers and sons, camels and pigs, coins and cloaks. A homily is most effective if the preacher sees his role as being a liaison between the people in the pews and our Almighty God.

This is a tall order to be sure. I don't hit a homerun every week. And let's face it, some people called to serve God in the ordained ministry will just not be as effective at preaching as others. If we look at the lives of the saints, we do see some who were renowned preachers, but others who are more known for their tender pastoral care or their mercy in the confessional. So, if your preacher isn't exactly Archbishop Fulton Sheen, my advice is to listen hard for at least one helpful takeaway. Plus, these days you've got plenty of options if the homily you heard in church didn't do much for you. Go online and listen to another homily on the same readings from a livestreamed Mass—either across town or from somewhere else in the world!

50. Why doesn't the Creed include anything about the Eucharist?

I'm kinda bothered by something: Why doesn't the Profession of Faith mention anything about the Eucharist, which is such a central belief for Catholics? Seems odd to leave it out.

Guy, in Toronto, Ontario, Canada

You make a good point. If the Eucharist is important enough to be called "the summit and source of our faith" as Catholics (see *CCC* 1324), one would think we would throw in at least a brief mention of it when publicly affirming the things we believe! If we were drawing up a list of important Catholic beliefs today, we probably would include, in addition to the Eucharist, the protection of life from conception to natural death, the dignity of the human person, the pope, Mary's immaculate conception, God's unbounded mercy, and so on. But we find none of those topics in the Profession of Faith. So you've asked a good question here. Let's begin by parsing what the Creed is and what it is not.

The Profession of Faith is not an A+ answer on an oral exam in theology class. It is not meant to be an exhaustive list of all, or even the most important, things that Catholics believe (even the eight-hundred-page *Catechism of the Catholic Church* on my desk does not purport to be an exhaustive treatise of all the teachings of the Church; it refers to itself as a summary!). Nor is the Creed akin to a corporate mission statement that hangs on the wall as a litmus test for every project we undertake.

What it is, is a prayer during Mass. Another less common term for the Creed or Profession of Faith is the *Symbolum*, a Latin word for "symbol." This prayer is a symbol of our faith. Symbols are partial representations of the broader realities they point to. A yellow triangle-shaped sign with an exclamation point on it likely communicates "caution," "danger," or possibly "steep cliff ahead," even though none of those words are printed on it. Think of how many ideas, words, or emotions are conveyed by that little wink emoji in a text. So it's not necessary that every tenet of faith be enumerated in the Creed. But what about what it does contain?

The Nicene-Constantinopolitan Creed, the one most commonly recited at Sunday Mass, is a formulation of beliefs drafted in the fourth century. It is almost entirely made up of statements about the three persons of the Blessed Trinity, and even follows the structure of Father-Son-Holy Spirit. There are a few additional short phrases at the end, but the lion's share of the text is about the Trinity. There are two primary reasons for this: one is theological/sacramental and the other historical/political.

Sacramentally, the first time any profession of faith is prayed in the life of a Christian is at his or her baptism. And we are baptized using what we call the *trinitarian formula*. "The symbol of faith is first and foremost the baptismal creed. Since baptism is given 'in the name of the Father and of the Son and of the Holy Spirit' the truths of faith professed during baptism are articulated in terms of their reference to the three persons of the Holy Trinity" (*CCC* 189). Furthermore, "The mystery of the Most Holy Trinity is the central mystery of Christian faith and life....*It is therefore the source of all the other mysteries of faith*, the light that enlightens them. It is the most fundamental and essential teaching in the 'hierarchy of the truths of faith'" (*CCC* 234, emphasis added). In other words, if we have limited time at Mass and need to choose some teaching to publicly profess as a *symbolum* of our entire faith, our go-to is the Trinity.

Historically, nearly all formulaic declarations of Christian faith arose out of a particular need or as a response to controversies, confusion, or heresies. When all the leaders of the Church met as a council in the ancient Greek city of Nicea in the year 325, one of the burning issues of the day was that a growing number of Christians were swayed by an opinion that Jesus wasn't really divine in the same way that God the Father is, and that he was created by God along with humans and other creatures. In response to this heresy (erroneous belief), the Council of Nicea vehemently affirmed Christ's divinity and his oneness with the Father. That's why every week we utter phrases like "true God from true God, begotten not made" and "consubstantial with the Father." Indeed, Nicea focused so much on Jesus that it took another sixty years before the part about the Holy Spirit was added to the Creed at the Council of Constantinople—hence, its full title is the Nicene-Constantinopolitan Creed.

Over the centuries, many different creeds were produced, often in response to other heresies or questions. The verbose Profession of the Faith of the Council of Trent—countering the objections of the Protestant Reformation of the sixteenth century—does in fact reference our belief in the Eucharist. "I also profess that...in the most holy sacrament of the Eucharist there is truly, really, and substantially present the body and blood together with the soul and the divinity of our Lord Jesus Christ, and that there takes place a conversion of the whole substance of bread into the body, and of the whole substance of the wine into the blood; and this conversion the Catholic Church calls transubstantiation" (Pope Pius IV, *Iniunctum Nobis*, 1565). That Profession of Trent (of which the above is only a portion) clocks in at nearly nine hundred words and contains additional paragraphs about Scripture and papal authority. Imagine standing to recite that every Sunday. We'd have to spread out the Mass times at the parish!

While there are multiple creeds in Catholic tradition, only a couple have been chosen for proclamation during Mass (see *CCC* 193; *GIRM* 67). And as with many things in the Church, doing something for a long time makes it stick. The Nicene Creed and the Apostles' Creed have pride of place not because either of them sums up everything we believe, but because Christians have been publicly reciting them for over a thousand years.

Yet even though we do not explicitly declare our belief in the Eucharist during the Profession of Faith, we certainly do in other ways throughout the Mass. The assembly's resounding "Amen" at the end of the Eucharistic Prayer, which included the priest saying "this is my body...this is my blood" is arguably a more powerful affirmation of our belief in the True Presence than if we were to add a line to the Creed.

PART 7

Posture, Gestures, and Ritual Actions

51. What's with all the calisthenics at Catholic Mass?

52. Are we supposed to genuflect or bow when coming into the church?

53. When carrying things, are we to bow toward the altar?

54. Should I be making the Sign of the Cross more often during Mass?

55. Why do we bow during the Profession of Faith?

56. Should we be kneeling or standing during the Eucharistic Prayer?

57. What happened to ringing the bells during Mass? **TOP 5**

58. Why does the priest get a larger host than the people do?

59. What do we do with our hands during the Our Father? **TOP 5**

60. How should we bow during the communion rite?

51. What's with all the calisthenics at Catholic Mass?

I'm not Catholic but I attend Mass with my wife. Can you explain to me why there is so much standing, sitting, and kneeling? I can't keep up. It reminds me of morning calisthenics with my company!

Dylan in Ft. Hood, Texas

Sounds like you're in the military, right Dylan? **Dylan:** Yessir.

Well then you might appreciate the reasons for all our up and down movements at Mass even more than most folks. You know that there are many ways you can feel an inner respect for a superior, but standing rigidly at attention and saluting is a full-body expression of that respect—plus it's a lot harder to be distracted by other things while maintaining that posture, isn't it? When you march in lockstep or line up in formation, it doesn't merely look good, it is a powerful demonstration that all those serving are united with a common purpose, and under a single authority. Let me even double down on that: when everyone in your unit takes the same stance, it not only displays an inner camaraderie that you feel with one another, it in fact *makes* you more unified because it's physical, visual, more "real." In Catholic terms, we would say that it both symbolizes and brings about unity among you.

At an even more basic level, people of many religions value the role of the body in prayer. Jews stand up and bow back and forth while praying at the Western Wall in Jerusalem. Muslims orient their bodies in the direction of Mecca, their holiest city, while crouching down on a mat on the floor five times a day for their prayer. Not to mention yoga! It may seem like a thoroughly modern thing to be aware of the body-mind-spirit connection. In reality, people of faith have been embracing that for millennia.

Our master document that directs us how to celebrate Catholic Mass declares, "The gestures and posture of the priest, the deacon, and the ministers, as well as those of the people, ought to contribute to making the entire celebration resplendent with beauty and noble simplicity, so that the true and full meaning of the different parts of the celebration is evident and that the participation of all is fostered" (*GIRM* 42). There are a couple of more reasons for you, Dylan: our various changes in posture accentuate the meaning of what we are doing and encourage everyone to be active participants, rather than an audience, during Mass.

Sitting is a receptive, listening position used while the Scripture readings are proclaimed or the homily is preached. Standing is an expression of respect (just like in the military), so we stand at important times like when the cross is being processed into church, or when we're professing the Creed together. Kneeling is an ancient embodiment of humility and reverence before a divine or royal authority. Therefore we kneel when the presence of Christ our King comes into our midst during the Eucharistic Prayer. There's a purpose and meaning to every movement.

Dylan: That makes a lot of sense. Thank you, sir.

52. Are we supposed to genuflect or bow when coming into the church?

When I visit Catholic churches other than my own, sometimes I see people bowing when they first come in rather than genuflecting like we do at my parish. Which is correct?

Beth in Great Falls, Montana

First of all, we neither genuflect nor bow to the church space in general. So what you do when you first arrive at Mass may depend on the arrangement of the church. Let's begin with this: one genuflects toward the tabernacle but bows to the altar. If you're in a church where the tabernacle is directly behind the altar in the sanctuary area, you need not do both. Just think of the tabernacle as "outranking" the altar and genuflect.

But differing architecture complicates the matter. Some churches reserve the Blessed Sacrament in a separate side chapel that may be neither near nor directly in line with the main altar in the front. You may be less familiar with this design, but it is used in all four Major Basilicas in Rome, including St. Peter's, as well as the Basilica of the National Shrine of the Immaculate Conception in Washington, D.C., and many cathedrals around the world. Also, if a parish has committed to perpetual adoration of the Blessed Sacrament, they may have a smaller chapel distinct from the main church that has its own door to the outside so that people may come and go at all hours, oftentimes using a code to enter when the main church is locked overnight. In any of these cases, it would be most appropriate to make a reverent bow in the direction of the altar rather than twisting your body in some different direction to genuflect.

However, even though many Catholics do make some gesture of reverence as soon as they walk in the door of their church, strictly speaking, we're not required to do that. The *General Instruction of the Roman Missal* dictates that the ministers should make a profound bow at the end of the entrance procession "on reaching the altar" (*GIRM* 122), and that anyone who "passes in front of" the Blessed Sacrament should genuflect (*GIRM* 274). Nei-

mass class notes

Adoration: spending time in quiet prayer in front of the consecrated Eucharist

ther of these sound like something we're all supposed to do in the entranceway, or even upon arriving at our pew several rows back from the altar. Although the Church does not specify how close you need to be to the tabernacle to genuflect, there is something to be said for proximity, particularly in a large worship space. Allow me to play devil's advocate for a moment (and please don't think me glib or disrespectful; my point will emerge shortly): Why not genuflect when you get out of your car in the church parking lot? You know the Blessed Sacrament is just inside; the walls surely don't block the presence of the Lord. Or maybe you have to be able to *see* the tabernacle? In that case, should you genuflect immediately upon catching sight of it after walking through the front door? Not according to the *General Instruction*. It says that when "the tabernacle with the Most Blessed Sacrament is present in the sanctuary, the priest, the deacon, and the other ministers genuflect *when they approach the altar* and when they depart from it" (*GIRM* 274, emphasis added). What this means in practice is that the bishop, priest, or other ministers begin their procession at the back of church, move up the main aisle, but they do not genuflect until they reach the foot of the altar steps. That is, until they get *closer* to the tabernacle.

The ritual action we call a genuflection is similar to the age-old tradition of humbly kneeling in the presence of a monarch. In medieval times, when someone were to address the king in person, they would first enter a large hall, walk up a long aisle with members of the court flanking on both sides, and then when they reached the steps of the throne where the king was seated, they would make a deep bow or go down on one knee in humility before the king. But they didn't make that sign of reverence when they first walked in the big hall. They waited until they got face-to-face with the monarch.

I don't bring this up to argue that we stop genuflecting in church and thus exhibit less reverence for the Blessed Sacrament. In fact my point is just the opposite. Maybe you've heard stories of Catholics who were so conditioned to genuflecting in the aisle just before entering their desired pew that they unthinkingly do the same at movie theaters or school assemblies. I doubt the medieval commoner who knelt before his king in court made a similar mistake in the marketplace later that day. Picture, also, a whole family showing up to Mass. Upon arriving at their favorite pew, they each genuflect in something of a hurry because everybody is bunching up in the aisle waiting to get in and sit down. Some might respond that doing it like that is better than no expression of reverence whatsoever. And I hear that.

My concern is that when we do something so frequently out of habit it can become perfunctory and devoid of its true meaning.

POSTURE, GESTURES, AND RITUAL ACTIONS

Genuflecting is meant to show a profound sense of adoration of and humility before our Lord. It is an ancient posture of worshiping God (see Psalm 95:6; Daniel 6:10; Revelation 19:10). I think we lose sense of that with a half-hearted curtsy made at the front door.

So here's my recommendation. When you first walk into a Catholic Church, look around and figure out where the Blessed Sacrament is. Then make a short trip over there. Genuflect, or if there is a kneeler, kneel down and spend a moment in quiet prayer. Then make your way back to your pew. I try to do this when I'm visiting a church I've not been to before. In my opinion, a practice like this will do a better job reinforcing our belief about Christ's True Presence in the Eucharist than any cursory bodily action we make when we cross the threshold of the church doors.

53. When carrying things, are we to bow toward the altar?

My teen son is an altar server. I'm proud of him since he really seems to know what he's doing and is graceful and composed up there. One thing seems odd to me, though. Because he's the tallest, they always have him carrying the processional cross at the beginning and end of Mass. He reaches the altar first and waits for the priest and other ministers to line up, and then they all make a deep bow to the altar. It looks weird to me for him to bow while holding the cross like that. Is that right?

Roberta in Columbus, Ohio

Ah, finally…an easy question! I'm happy to hear you find your son to be graceful on the altar. That's no small task. But, no, anyone carrying important things in a procession should not genuflect or even make a profound bow (from the waist). They are instructed to only make a simple bow of the head (*GIRM* 274). The reason why they are holding these liturgical "props" high (like an acolyte with the cross, altar servers with candles, or the deacon holding

159

aloft the Book of the Gospels) is to draw attention to them for the sake of the assembly. These are symbols of Christ in our midst, so the ministers are giving an opportunity for the people in the pews to show reverence. It defeats the purpose if the minister diminishes that while expressing their own reverence toward the altar or tabernacle. Not to mention the scenarios that may unfold if someone carrying a lit candle was to bow deeply! Wax everywhere. Hair catching on fire…don't get me started. So the Church wisely makes an adjustment for these ministerial and practical concerns by allowing a bow of the head for processional ministers.

Similarly, a family who has been chosen to bring up the gifts of bread and wine as the altar is prepared should not genuflect or make a deep bow while they're carrying those items. Think of the potential for spillage! Typically the way this plays out is that the people carrying up the gifts hand them to the priest or deacon or altar server first and then make a bow to the altar before turning and returning to their pew.

mass class notes

Liturgical: having to do with public ritual celebrations

As an aside, this would not apply to anyone who has *anything* in their hands while in a Church procession. Many people, including the priest, often have a hymnal or printed song sheet while walking up the aisle. There's no exemption from a genuflection or profound bow just because you're holding a music reference.

But your son does get a pass. You can tell him that he can keep the cross vertical and held high and merely bow his head while others are making more demonstrative signs of reverence. It's okay because he's serving an important role at that moment.

54. Should I be making the Sign of the Cross more often during Mass?

Some people during Mass make the Sign of the Cross a lot more than others do. After we call to mind our sins and receive forgiveness, I see some people make the Sign of the Cross. At communion time, some people make a Sign of the Cross after receiving the host. Should I be doing this? Should they?

Charlene in Wichita, Kansas.

Unless the number of times you currently make the Sign of the Cross during Mass is *one*, no, you need not do it more frequently. There are only two instances where the ritual calls for all in the gathered assembly to make the Sign of the Cross. And these are both pretty obvious: at the beginning and end of Mass (*GIRM* 124, 167). Both times the presiding priest or bishop makes it quite clear that the assembly is to do this as he actually says aloud, "Father, Son, and Holy Spirit," while extending his right hand and similarly making the Sign of the Cross directed toward the people. So when all that happens, you should go ahead and cross yourself. Doing so at other times throughout the Mass is not necessary—but not a crime!

I'm guessing that some of the folks you notice crossing themselves more often are in what we might call an "older demographic." That makes sense because the people in the pews did in fact used to make the Sign of the Cross more often during Mass prior to the changes made in 1970. Habits like that are hard to break. Beyond that, the two examples you gave are fairly common in people of all ages. Here's why I think that's the case.

During the first part of Mass, the Penitential Act (calling to mind our sins, as you said) concludes with the priest praying aloud, "May almighty God have mercy on us, forgive us our sins, and bring us to everlasting life." This is when you notice many people crossing themselves. Likely it's because this reminds them of what happens toward the end of the sacrament of reconciliation (confession): the priest offers absolution with the blessing, "I absolve you from your sins, in the name of the Father, and of the Son, and of the Holy Spirit," while making the Sign of the Cross over the penitent. While the priest's blessing at the end of the Penitential Act at Mass is similar—in fact, the *Roman Missal* even calls it the "absolution"—since he neither says aloud nor makes the Sign of the Cross, neither does the assembly. Again, it is very understandable why people would instinctively cross themselves at this point, and there's nothing wrong with doing that. But your question is, do you need to do that? No, you do not.

The other example you gave happens during communion. Crossing oneself after receiving communion is not prescribed by our *Roman Missal*. But it's probably just another one of those actions that "just feels right." It is a powerful, reverent moment and making the Sign of the Cross probably happens without thinking about it. In a sense, that's good. It indicates that what just happened is sacred and not just another daily task. Even I did that ever since I was a kid up until the time I became a priest. Again, it's not a sin if you do it, but you do not have to.

Should I be making the Sign of the Cross more often?

Restricting the action of making the Sign of the Cross to the very beginning and end of Mass reinforces that everything contained between those two gestures is *one* liturgical action, one celebration of the Eucharist, rather than lots of smaller rituals strung together.

55. Why do we bow during the Profession of Faith?

I've always wondered why we bow at a certain point during the recitation of the Creed. Can you shed some light on this for me?

Gary, driving on I-10 in Arizona

I'm happy to. Let's first look at exactly when during the Creed we bow so that we may better understand why we do it. The Church asks us all to bow during this line in the Nicene Creed: "...and by the Holy Spirit was incarnate of the Virgin Mary, and became man." In the Apostles' Creed the phrasing is, "...who was conceived by the Holy Spirit, born of the Virgin Mary...." We are instructed to make a *profound* bow here, which means it is a bow from the waist, not a simple bow of the head. This indicates that whatever we're saying is "kind of a big deal," to quote Ron Burgundy from the movie *Anchorman*.

So why bow during these words? Does it mean that part of the Creed is the most important part? Not exactly. But those words are describing one of the all-time most significant events for those who believe in Christ. We might typically refer to Jesus being born as Christmas. Theologically, though, the proper term is the *incarnation*. This is the moment in human history when God the Creator of the universe, who has no beginning or end, chose to become one of us, to take on our flesh, to be truly "God…with us" (Matthew 1:23). Prior to that, the world was broken and in need of healing, in need of a savior. Then, "the Word became flesh and made his dwelling among us" (John 1:14). This is not merely another blip on a religious timeline; this is the pivotal point for the salvation of all humanity. It *is* a big deal. The Church teaches that "belief in the true Incarnation of the Son of God is the distinctive sign of Christian faith" (*CCC* 463). We bow so as to offer witness, with our very bodies, to the profundity of this momentous act.

In fact, twice a year we even ramp up our show of reverence a little further. At Christmas Masses and on the Feast of the Annunciation (March 25), we *kneel down* during the line when the Creed mentions the incarnation (*GIRM* 137).

Here's a take on this that makes sense to me. The incarnation can be thought of as the moment that Christ appears to us for the first time, or in theatrical parlance, his grand entrance. There are times in our life when somebody's entrance elicits a change in our posture. When a person of importance enters the room, often those who've been awaiting their arrival stand up as a sign of respect. In the legal arena, the bailiff announces, "All rise!" as the judge makes his or her entrance into the courtroom. Since we're already standing as we recite the Creed, we exhibit a different posture change when speaking of Jesus's grand entrance into the story of humanity.

56. Should we be kneeling or standing during the Eucharistic Prayer?

While visiting my daughter in another state, we attended a Catholic Mass where the entire congregation remained standing throughout the Eucharistic Prayer. I've never seen this. Aren't we supposed to be kneeling for that part of the Mass? I kept wondering if I should kneel down just by myself. I didn't, but it still felt weird to stand.

Kathi Ann in Arlington, Virginia

Let me start by saying, you did the right thing by standing along with everybody else. But let's unpack what happened and why it seemed so unfamiliar to you. First of all, you are correct that usually the assembly assumes the posture of kneeling during the entirety of the Eucharistic Prayer. That's what you're used to and that is in fact the norm in the United States these days.

The *General Instruction of the Roman Missal* says, "In the dioceses of the United States of America, (the faithful) should kneel beginning after the singing or recitation of the Sanctus until after the Amen of the Eucharistic Prayer, except when prevented on occasion by reasons of health, lack of space, the large number of people present, or some other good reason" (no. 43). Seems clear enough, but it's always helpful to look at the broader context.

First of all, the name of this guiding document, sort of our master plan for how we celebrate Mass throughout the Universal Church, is telling. It is meant to be "general" and an "instruction." It is *general* in the sense that the Church intends this to be the baseline but also allows for local adaptation and inculturation of these general norms. An entire chapter of the *General Instruction* (nos. 386–99) is devoted to how bishops' conferences (essentially bishops of a national area) and each diocesan bishop may go about tailoring the norms to be most appropriate for their faithful. Further, the *General Instruction* contains instructions not laws. It's not called the "Laws for Correctly Celebrating Mass." Because the Mass is an event enacted and embodied by diverse human people, there is intentional latitude built into the instructions.

Another broad context is that we are a global Church. Because of the aforementioned intended local adaptations of the general norms, one will have a slightly different experience of the ritual of Mass in different parts of the world. Watch any televised papal Mass from the time of Pope St. John Paul II to the present, and you will likely notice things that you've never seen at your local parish on Sunday. And that's not only allowed, it's what is intended! Of course, there is a delicate balance to be struck between the familiarity and universality of the Mass and its local inculturation. But that balance must be discerned by people (bishops, pastors, ministers) implementing the general instructions the Church offers. In terms of your question, if you go to Mass while traveling in Europe, you will notice less kneeling: in some countries or dioceses they stand throughout the Eucharistic Prayer; in others they kneel only around the consecration. In Canada, in fact, the practice of kneeling or standing during the Eucharistic Prayer differs from that of the United States—and even varies in different Canadian dioceses.

All of these local adaptations have been approved by the Vatican, so the variety is just part of life as a Catholic.

Certainly this rubs up against our desire for consistency. We'd prefer things to be the same everywhere. Recently, when driving a rented car in Italy, I was thrown off by the fact that parking spaces painted with blue paint are intended for regular metered parking, whereas here in the United States, a blue parking space universally means it is designated parking only for people with a handicapped tag. You can imagine I drove around a lot looking for nonblue spaces! But once I became familiar with the different signage, I was able to adapt (and park).

Finally, a bit of historical context. Catholics up through the Middle Ages stood during the entire Mass as their sign of respect and reverence for the sacrament. In fact, for a period of time, kneeling was considered a penitential act and thus not appropriate for Sundays. This did not prevail, however, and kneeling during certain parts of the Mass has been the standard for roughly one thousand years. Until 1970! The first edition of the *General Instruction of the Roman Missal* that went into effect right after the reforms of the Second Vatican Council indicated that in the United States people should stand throughout the Eucharistic Prayer, only kneeling at the words of consecration. So for about forty years, new churches were built, and old ones redesigned, that did not even have kneelers. Some dioceses and even individual parishes still held to the custom of kneeling, but overall practice was mixed at best.

Over time, the reaction to this on the part of many American Catholics was that even when kneeling wasn't mandated, it just

mass class notes

Consecration: a sacred blessing, or specifically the part of the Mass when the priest prays the words Christ used at the Last Supper didn't feel right "in our gut" not to do so. It's also such an identifiably *Catholic* posture to be kneeling during prayer that maybe it just doesn't seem to some people "Catholic enough" unless we're kneeling. This is perhaps what you experienced when you visited a different parish that was standing during the Eucharistic Prayer.

Partly because of this, in 2003, when a revised edition of the *General Instruction* was issued from Rome, the U.S. Bishops requested that our local adaptation be to return to kneeling during the whole Eucharistic Prayer as the normative practice in the American Church. Hence the language I quoted above in *GIRM* 43. There are notable exceptions of course. In April 2008, when Pope Benedict XVI visited the United States, he celebrated a huge outdoor Mass at Nationals Park in Washington, D.C. I was there covering the event as part of a broadcast team from the Catholic Channel on SiriusXM. I noticed that in the printed worship aid for the Mass there was an advisory that due to being in a baseball stadium without kneelers, the faithful should express their reverence by standing throughout the Eucharistic Prayer. This squarely fits into the exceptions listed in the *General Instruction*: "except when prevented on occasion by reasons of health, lack of space, the large number of people present, or some other good reason."

But wait…aren't we now right back where we started? When you visited that other Catholic Church, you were in the United States, it was after 2003, and you weren't in an open-air baseball stadium. So why weren't they kneeling?!

I don't know for sure. But I do know that because standing was normative for about two generations, some parishes were able to return to the posture of kneeling quicker than others. Indeed, a good number of churches were designed and constructed in that time without kneelers. In some cases it's not as simple as running to the church supply store and buying kneelers when the new *General Instruction* is issued. Funds may need to be raised, habits changed, and hearts transformed. That's why the instruction about kneeling allows for exceptions to the norm "for a good reason."

And guess who gets to determine if a reason is good enough? "The diocesan Bishop, who is to be regarded as the high priest of his flock...must promote, regulate, and be vigilant over the liturgical life in his diocese" (*GIRM* 387). So we have to presume (and it's a good bet in this age of instant communication) that the bishop of the diocese where you visited that church knows what is going on and has (at least tacitly) approved this.

But now we come to the most important part of your question. That is, *would it have been right for you to choose to kneel in the midst of an all-standing congregation during the Eucharistic Prayer?* We've already said that kneeling is the norm in the United States and the *General Instruction* says it's what the faithful *should* do. Yet we also are taught this by the *General Instruction*:

> In the celebration of Mass the faithful form a holy people, a people whom God has made his own....They should, moreover, endeavor to make this clear by their deep religious sense and their charity toward brothers and sisters who participate with them in the same celebration. Thus, *they are to shun any appearance of individualism or division.* Indeed, they form one body.... *This unity is beautifully apparent from the gestures and postures observed in common by the faithful.* (*GIRM* 95–96, emphasis added)

In point of fact, the Church spends a great deal more time exhorting us to be united, even with our posture, than it does prescribing kneeling during the Eucharistic Prayer. That's why I said you made the right choice by standing.

You may have heard the age-old saying "When in Rome, do as the Romans do." What you may not know is that this originally was specifically referring to ritual practice during Mass. Before everyone on the planet was connected by the internet, it was harder for people to keep up with what was going on in other countries, or even other cities in the same country. Hundreds of years ago, Catholics in Milan, for instance, had established different rituals used during the celebration of Mass than people in Rome. When they would travel, they would be surprised by these differences, and as you experienced, their temptation was to hold fast to the practice with which they were most familiar. This caused disruption during the Mass. So the Universal Church advanced the notion of the *inculturation* of the Mass with the maxim, "When in Rome, do as the Romans do." Implied is the converse, "When in Milan, do as the Milanese do." This is still in force today.

So if you visit a Catholic Church somewhere in the world where they do something unusual you've never experienced before, go with it. It may be very appropriate for you to inquire after Mass with the pastor or another minister as to why they do that at their church. It may even be so radical that it warrants you complaining in writing to their bishop. But during Mass is not the time to object by striking a posture contrary to what others around you are doing. The uniformity of posture of the faithful gathered *at this Mass* takes precedence over any desired ritual consistency throughout the diocese or country.

Ultimately, the Mass is in no way a private prayer experience of an individual Catholic. Mass is *we* not *me*.

57. What happened to ringing the bells during Mass?

When I was an altar boy–I won't tell you how long ago–
I was trained to ring the bells at certain points during
the Mass. Why did they take them away? I miss hearing
them.

Angelo in Manchester, New Hampshire

Ah, the bells! You're not alone, Angelo. I've heard a lot of Catholics say they miss the bells. Plenty of others still get to hear the bells, though, because some parishes have retained the practice of ringing them. Since the liturgical reforms of the Second Vatican Council, ringing bells during Mass is no longer a required ritual action—but it is still allowed (*GIRM* 150).

Ringing bells during the consecration of the Eucharistic elements served a practical purpose in the Mass as we used to celebrate it prior to 1970. Imagine you're a parishioner sitting fifty yards back in a large church before the invention of sound amplifiers. Then imagine the priest is praying the Eucharistic Prayer in a language you do not understand (Latin). And on top of that, he has his back to you and he's doing some actions you can't see because his body is blocking whatever is going on. At best you could make out unintelligible murmurings for fifteen to twenty minutes. Must have been hard to stay focused. In fact many people didn't even try. Often they would resort to praying the rosary or quietly saying some other devotional prayers they knew in their native tongue while the Latin murmuring was going on way up there on the altar. But people did want to be alerted to when the "important part" was happening. So bells were rung just before the consecration so the people wouldn't miss it.

Then came Vatican II with its strong emphasis on full, active, and conscious participation on the part of the entire gathered assembly during all of the Mass. The thinking was, now that the people in the pews can understand what is being prayed in their own language, and they can hear it better with the aid of microphones, and even visually pay attention to the action more easily because the priest is facing in their direction and not obscuring the eucharistic elements, they surely will not need a bell rung to know when the consecration is happening.

So the bells are no longer needed for that purpose. But some parishes still ring them as a means of highlighting a very meaningful and significant moment in the Mass. Incense is still used in this way as well, playing on the sense of smell and sight. The bells are an auditory way to enhance and bring greater solemnity to a high point of the Mass. And let's face it: just because we can understand the language Mass is prayed in does not mean we are immune to a touch of mind wandering or daydreaming. I've heard some people say the bells "call them back" to a sharper focus and they like that. I've also heard people describe it as a kind of act of worship in itself, almost like a brief moment of musical praise.

Bottom line, parishes may choose to ring the bells at the consecration, or they may forgo the practice. If you miss them, Angelo, it can't hurt to mention that to your pastor. Maybe he's got a deep-seated reason for not using bells. But who knows? Maybe he misses them too. I kinda do.

58. Why does the priest get a larger host than the people do?

I have to say, Father Dave, I've often wondered why the priest gets a bigger host for communion than we people in the pews.

Evelyn in Bellevue, Washington

It sounds like I should start off by saying that it's *not* because the priest is holier or deserving of more of the sacrament. So, it doesn't stem from clericalism. Nor do we believe the Eucharist can be quantified, and thus someone who consumes a larger piece of the consecrated host or takes a bigger drink from the chalice does not get any more grace from the sacrament than anyone else. The reasons for the size difference all have to do with ritual celebration.

There are actually three different sizes of hosts. The ones you in the assembly typically consume are roughly one-inch in diameter. Then there's a three-inch host and a six-inch host. It might be either one of these that you're seeing the priest use at Mass. Why does he get the bigger ones?

Think of a teacher up in front of a classroom using a big thick black dry-erase marker on a large white board. She might be writing the same words or math formulas as the students using smaller pens and paper at their desks, but we wouldn't think to ourselves, "Hey, how come she gets to use a larger pen and writing surface?" That wouldn't cross our minds because we understand she needs her implements to be larger so that everyone in the class can see what she's writing. Would we expect her, out of some sense of egalitarianism, to use a regular Bic pen and single sheet of loose-leaf paper to teach? Of course not.

After the words of consecration are said by the priest, the *Roman Missal* directs, "He shows the consecrated host to the people, places it again on the paten, and genuflects in adoration." This is so all those gathered at Mass may worship in adoration of Christ's presence in the Blessed Sacrament. If the priest is supposed to show the host to the people, it had better be big enough for the people to actually see it, even all the way in the last pew. Hence, three-inch host for chapels and smaller churches; six-inch host for cathedrals and other large churches where the altar may be far away from the people.

We do the same thing with other items at Mass. The processional cross carried by an acolyte is larger than the one you wear around your neck. The Book of the Gospels held aloft in procession by a deacon is bigger and more ornate than the missalette you're reading the Scripture from in your pew. All of these things are larger for the sake of the people in the assembly and because rituals are inherently visual.

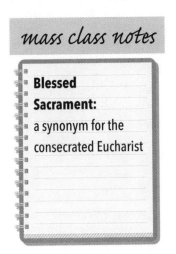

mass class notes

Blessed Sacrament: a synonym for the consecrated Eucharist

In fact, the large six-inch host is perforated so the priest can break it up into smaller pieces and mix those in with the other round hosts, so that a few of the people receiving communion actually consume a part of the one big host as well.

Finally, some may be old enough to remember the concept of "ocular communion." Because for a long period in the Church's history few people received communion with any frequency, at most Masses they would remain behind in the pews when communion time came. For them, the next best option was communing with the Lord by gazing upon his True Presence in the Eucharist when the priest held up the consecrated host—a spiritual practice known as ocular communion. If he used the small one-inch host for that, we could probably call it "squinting communion."

59. What do we do with our hands during the Our Father?

Father Dave, I dislike it when a stranger tries to hold my hand while praying the Our Father during Mass. Thankfully, we don't do this anymore. But now I see people raising their hands up in the air. Are we all supposed to be doing that?

Darryl in Edmonton, Alberta, Canada

Even though this is one of the most common questions we've received in all the years of being on the radio, it is probably the one that I have the least satisfying answer for. Bottom line is that the Church has no stance on what our stance should be during the Lord's Prayer. (I think I just made a dad joke.) It would be more accurate to say that there are no directions as to what to do or not do with our *hands*. The *General Instruction* merely tells us to be standing (see *GIRM* 43).

Although the COVID-19 pandemic pretty much eliminated the practice of joining hands for the Our Father, it was a grassroots custom that took hold in the United States in the decades following the Second Vatican Council. No official Church document ever legislated it; it was something that people just did. And because many Catholic traditions do arise from the piety and practice of the People of God, it was not squelched by the hierarchy. Some people really loved grabbing the hands of their family members and fellow parishioners during the Lord's Prayer. But many, like you, were not big fans of this touchy-feely prayer posture.

There have been theological critiques as well. An entire congregation joining hands together (in some cases even spanning the church aisle) is a powerful visual symbol of individual people coming together in unity. True, this is one of the most salient things we pray for during the Mass, but not *primarily* during the Lord's Prayer. To single out, with a dramatic change in communal posture, the Our Father as the sole unifying moment in the Mass belies the myriad other prayers and rituals that implore God to bring us together as one, such as, "Grant that we, who are nourished by the Body and Blood of your Son and filled with his Holy Spirit, may become one body, one spirit in Christ" (Eucharistic Prayer III). Those words seem more suited to accompany the action of hand holding than the words of the Lord's Prayer.

Another custom has emerged in more recent years: that of the congregation extending both hands with palms facing upward during the recitation of the Lord's Prayer. This posture has also been criticized by some who think it too similar to the *orans* position of the priest leading the community in prayer with hands raised. While there is merit in discouraging the members of the assembly from mimicking every posture used by the priest, it is also true that in the earliest centuries of the Church's history the people did in fact stand praying with hands outstretched during much of the Mass.

So the jury is still out on this. For now, it comes down to the local custom of your parish. And while unified posture is important during Mass, this is one instance where I'd say if you don't feel comfortable raising your hands up in the air, you needn't feel obligated to do so.

60. How should we bow during the communion rite?

What is the bow at communion supposed to be like? Is it just a head nod, as I see some people do?

Frannie in Hamburg, New York

I am so glad that you asked this, Frannie. Because going by what I see when I am distributing communion, there does not seem to be a single answer to "What is the bow supposed to be like?" Sometimes I feel like I am a judge on a televised talent show and as each new act walks onto the stage, I am surprised by their unique performance. Forgive my hyperbole, and please don't hear this as my blaming the People of God for this inconsistency. On the contrary, I believe the onus is on us ministers to educate people better about these things. To wit, we produced a video in our "Sacraments 101" series on BustedHalo.com trying to illustrate the proper way to receive communion, including the bow you're asking about. Maybe playing that video on a loop at the entrance to the church might help! But to answer you now, allow me to "zoom out" for a little perspective.

Prior to 1970, when American Catholics received communion, they would almost always be kneeling at an altar rail and extending their tongue. Since then, though, "the norm for reception of Holy Communion in the dioceses of the United States is standing....The consecrated host may be received either on the tongue or in the hand, at the discretion of each communicant" (*GIRM* 160). After living into this new practice for a few decades, it was felt that what was missing was an appropriate expression of reverence on the part of the communicant that is rightly due Christ's True Presence in the Eucharist. After all, it used to be "built in": upon reception of the sacrament, one would already be kneeling, a posture from time immemorial expressing humility, reverence, and honor. Without that, one could more easily succumb to the temptation to move through the line expediently as if lining up to grab free samples at Costco.

Thus, when the *Roman Missal* was updated in 2003, the Vatican left it up to the bishops of each country to determine an appropriate sign of reverence to be made by the communicant before receiving the Eucharist (*GIRM* 390). After considering various options, the U.S. Bishops settled on this: "When receiving Holy Communion, the communicant bows his or her head before the Sacrament as a gesture of reverence and receives the Body of the Lord from the minister" (*GIRM* 160).

Now we can address your question more specifically, Frannie. In Catholic ritual, there are two types of bows: *simple* and *profound*. A profound bow, also called a bow "of the body," is bowing from your waist. A simple bow is a bow of the head (see *GIRM* 275). Remember the term *fulcrum* from high school physics class? It's the bend point (like an elbow or knee). In a profound bow, the fulcrum is your waist. For a simple bow, the fulcrum is your neck. Why am I being so specific? Because so many people get this wrong, particularly in the communion line. The sign of reverence all American Catholics are asked to perform before receiving communion is *a simple bow of the head*.

You might wonder, "Why did the bishops not go with something grander, like the profound bow you've been talking about or even a genuflection?" Two reasons that I can think of. First, many gestures may be performed either in ways appropriate to a given situation or inappropriate. Imagine someone at Mass getting to the front of the communion line and doing something that looked more like a stage curtain call, where the actor dips way down then lurches back up, adding a flourish of his arm high in the air, saying, "Thank you, thank you very much!" I've seen people get pretty close to that in church, presumably thinking that the bigger the action, the more reverent it is. Not so. Conversely, just because something is "simple" does not mean it is irreverent or lacking in devotion. Don't forget one of the favorite mottoes of St. Teresa of Calcutta (Mother Teresa): "Do small things with great love." A bow of the head, done with great love, can be a powerful expression of reverence—as long as it is more than a perfunctory chin bob.

The other reason is that it appears that the bishops understand the practical dimensions of enacted ritual. What we do, how we pray when we gather for Mass, is not merely theoretical or spiritual. It has to work—humanly, logistically. We are not disembodied spirits. In my life before priesthood, I was a television director. Much of what a director does with actors and the crew is figure out "what works" in terms of camera angles, where set pieces go, and how the characters can move from one place to another. While not precisely the same, there is an analogy to what must be considered with regard to the postures, movements, and ritual actions during the Mass. Are those considerations more important than theological ones? No. But it's naive to think they don't matter at all.

Just picture, for instance, someone walking up to the priest, stopping about three feet away, extending their hands and bowing deeply from the waist—all in a single motion. Do you see in your mind's eye the communicant's hands dipping way down as they bow? It's like a fake out for the priest: the "target" for where I'm about to place the consecrated host has now become a moving target. I can't tell you how often I see this at Mass. Even without the hands extended, sometimes the person is so close to me when they bow that their head darn near knocks the plate of hosts out of my hands. Again, ritual needs to work—and that doesn't work. So, is a bow from the neck, where the hands don't really move at all, a better choice in that moment in the Mass? I'd say so.

What about kneeling or genuflecting, as I occasionally see some people do? There are those who are devout and also physically hearty enough to get down on the marble floor in front of the communion minister. However, without an altar rail and kneeler (most of these were removed after Vatican II), it should be evident that not everyone in the congregation would be able to achieve this physical feat—and if the Church wanted everyone to kneel down, we would have left the kneelers and altar rails in place. The U.S. Bishops chose as the universal sign of reverence at communion time a physical gesture that is possible for the vast majority of Catholics to perform: the simple bow. Although I was not in the room at the time of their decision, it is reasonable to deduce that the bishops made this choice not because the Eucharist deserves less reverence than kneeling symbolizes but because of the high value the Church places on the unity in posture of the entire assembly (see *GIRM* 95–96). True, expressions of reverence do vary throughout the world, but the Church does not leave the choice up to each individual Catholic at each Mass: "Attention should be paid to what is determined by this *General Instruction* and the traditional practice of the Roman Rite and to what serves the common spiritual good of the People of God, *rather than private inclination* or arbitrary choice" (*GIRM* 42, emphasis added). So while I appreciate that the occasional Catholic who kneels to receive communion apparently has a strong devotion to the True Presence of Christ in the Eucharist, the Church would like to remind him or her that the unity of the People of God is also of great importance. In fact, the *General Instruction*, as adapted for the United States, goes so far as to say, "Communicants should not be denied Holy Communion because they kneel. Rather, such instances should be addressed pastorally, by providing the faithful with proper catechesis on the reasons for this norm" (*GIRM* 160). Consider my answering this question an attempt to provide you with "proper catechesis" on this subject. Thanks for asking, Frannie!

Go! You Are Sent Forth....

There's a story of a second-grade religion teacher in a Catholic school who asked her class, "What is your favorite part of the Mass and why?"

After a moment of the usual blank stares, an eager Maria raised her hand and replied with a smile, "For me, it's when we read from the Bible because that's like God speaking directly to us."

The teacher affirmed her and looked around the room for other answers.

Tamara, usually shy, snuck her hand up. After waiting to be called on, she offered in a timid voice, "My favorite part is communion because that is when we receive Jesus into our bodies."

"A very good answer, Tamara. Anyone else?"

At that point, Timmy, known to be something of the class clown, blurted out, "I know, I know!" Reluctantly, the teacher allowed him to share. "The best part is at the very end when the priest says, 'The Mass is ended, go forth....'"

In an attempt to squelch the ensuing chuckles, the teacher chided with an eye roll, "Very funny, Timmy," regretting having taken a chance on the boy.

"No, I mean it!" he protested. "It *is* the best part. That's when we are told to bring Christ out into the world to everyone we meet.

Isn't that what it's all about? I mean, we're not sitting through the whole Mass just for our own sakes, right? We are supposed to share the love of God with other people, aren't we? How can we do that unless the priest sends us out?"

Finding it hard to argue with Timmy's enthusiasm, not to mention his theology, the teacher's face softened as she replied, "I see your point, Timmy. Thank you for reminding us of the importance of that final element of the Mass."

After soaking in her endorsement for a beat, Timmy added, "I also like the end of Mass because I no longer have to listen to my dad singing off key."

The Concluding Rites of the Mass are not merely another version of the bell that rings at the end of the school day. When the priest or deacon enjoins the assembly, "Go forth," it should not be heard as, "Okay folks, time to clear out. We gotta make room for the next group coming in." It should rather be taken more like a coach's last few words in the locker room before sending his team out onto the field: "Let's go get 'em!" It's the difference between referring to the ceremony at the end of your college years as "graduation" versus calling it "commencement." The latter denotes *this is not an end but a beginning.* All those hours in the classroom taking notes, all the studying for exams, all the double-spaced pages of term papers, can now be put to good use by heading out into the working world to contribute to society. Viewed this way, every part of the Mass leads to and culminates in the sending forth rite at the end. So in a very real sense, Timmy was right.

Since this book is called *Mass Class*, I would be remiss if I didn't point out that the most common word we use to describe our liturgical celebration of the Eucharist, *Mass*, is taken from Timmy's favorite part of it. For centuries, the Mass's closing words in Latin were *Ite, missa est*, "Go, you are sent forth...." Today, we use *Mass* as a noun describing a Catholic worship service—even in other languages: *misa* in Spanish, *messa* in Italian, *messe* in French. In that Latin command, however, it's a verb meaning to be sent forth with a purpose. It serves as the origin of words like *mission*, *commission*, *missionary*, and *dismissal*. Over time, Catholics chose to use this one word as a name for the entire celebration. Why? We don't know for sure. But there's an argument to be made that it's because the sending forth truly is the most important part.

The dismissal is a commencement. Or more accurately, a *commission*, not unlike that of Jesus to his followers right before he ascended into heaven: "Go, therefore, and make disciples of all nations, baptizing them in the name of the Father, and of the Son, and of the Holy Spirit, teaching them to observe all that I have commanded you. And behold, I am with you always, until the end of the age" (Matthew 28:19–20). During Mass, we've been trained, challenged, strengthened, and inspired. Now it's time to get out there and get to work! This commissioning extends the Mass beyond the walls of the church and well past the one hour we've spent together. We are called to pattern ourselves and our world after what we've just heard and experienced; to be so transformed by the Word of God and the sacrament of salvation that we actually have an impact on those we encounter; to "glorify the Lord with our lives," as one of the options for the words of dismissal puts it.

This can seem daunting, even scary, just as Christ's final words to those original disciples must have. But "behold, I am with you always," he reminds us. If that's true, what choice do we have? If we really believe we're walking down the street alongside Jesus, how could we not want to introduce him to everyone we meet? If during Mass I have just taken his True Presence inside my very body, how could I be so selfish as to keep him all to myself?

Without the concluding rites, it would be far too easy to view the Mass as a kind of spiritual spin class where we show up, sweat a little, get fueled and encouraged for our own self betterment, and then just, well...leave. Doesn't it seem a waste to spend four or five years in college studying in your major subject area only to end up not using it at all in your work life? Wouldn't it seem preposterous if, following the rousing halftime pep talk in the locker room, all the football players said, "Thanks coach" on their way out, and then just got in their cars and went to brunch? Of course it would. Yet most Catholics don't seem to have a problem treating Mass that way.

"See ya next week, Father," I often hear.

Yes, I hope so. But the real question is, How will you let this Mass we've just celebrated come alive this week for you, your family, and all those you encounter? *Ite, missa est.* You've been commissioned. Now go forth and bring Christ into your world!